SUBSIDIZING INEFFICIENCY

SUBSIDIZING INEFFICIENCY

A Study of State Aid and Local Government Productivity

By
Richard H. Silkman
and
Dennis R. Young
With the Assistance of Robert Lipp

PRAEGER

PRAEGER SPECIAL STUDIES • PRAEGER SCIENTIFIC

New York • Philadelphia • Eastbourne, UK
Toronto • Hong Kong • Tokyo • Sydney

Library of Congress Cataloging in Publication Data

Silkman, Richard H.
Subsidizing inefficiency.

Bibliography: p.
Includes index.
1. Grants-in-aid—United States—States.
2. State-local relations—United States.
3. Government productivity—United States.
4. Local government—United States. I. Young, Dennis R., 1943- . II. Lipp, Robert. III. Title.
HJ275.S53 1985 336.1'85 84-26628
ISBN 0-03-000662-7 (alk. paper)

Published in 1985 by Praeger Publishers
CBS Educational and Professional Publishing, a Division of CBS Inc.
521 Fifth Avenue, New York, NY 10175 USA

56789 052 987654321

Printed in the United States of America on acid-free paper

INTERNATIONAL OFFICES

Orders from outside the United States should be sent to the appropriate address listed below. Orders from areas not listed below should be placed through CBS International Publishing, 383 Madison Ave., New York, NY 10175 USA

Australia, New Zealand
Holt Saunders, Pty, Ltd., 9 Waltham St., Artarmon, N.S.W. 2064, Sydney, Australia

Canada
Holt, Rinehart & Winston of Canada, 55 Horner Ave., Toronto, Ontario, Canada M8Z 4X6

Europe, the Middle East, & Africa
Holt Saunders, Ltd., 1 St. Anne's Road, Eastbourne, East Sussex, England BN21 3UN

Japan
Holt Saunders, Ltd., Ichibancho Central Building, 22-1 Ichibancho, 3rd Floor, Chiyodaku, Tokyo, Japan

Hong Kong, Southeast Asia
Holt Saunders Asia, Ltd., 10 Fl, Intercontinental Plaza, 94 Granville Road, Tsim Sha Tsui East, Kowloon, Hong Kong

Manuscript submissions should be sent to the Editorial Director, Praeger Publishers, 521 Fifth Avenue, New York, NY 10175 USA

To Lynne and Rosalie

FOREWORD

The structure of grants-in-aid is central to the delivery of public services in this country. Grants from the federal government to states and localities, and from the states to local government, shape citizens' perceptions of the costs of service provision and create incentives for local officials to deliver services efficiently or inefficiently.

Despite the importance of grants, research regarding them has gotten side-tracked on a narrow aspect of their impact: their effect on local spending levels. Because spending data are the only pieces of information readily available, economists have tended to ask only the analytical questions that these data would fit.

It is the virtue of this book that the authors go beyond dollars spent to look at the actual services provided through the public sector -- such as the number of books circulated through public libraries and the hours these books are in use, or the number of children transported and the distances travelled through public school busing. They examine the effect of the grants system on the efficiency with which local governments produce the services that citizens recognize and value.

The results open new ground, both for policy understanding and for future analysis. Silkman and Young offer the first convincing evidence that the conservative critique of the grants structure is based on fact. Reliance on external aid to provide local services seems to push local government further and further from the efficiency frontier. Inefficiencies show up most conspicuously in the use and remuneration of labor. Under some conditions, the inefficiencies induced by the grants-in-aid system may be so large that categorical grants, despite stimulating spending, stimulate no real improvement in local service.

These findings may strengthen the case of a revamping of federalism so that every level of government is more directly and plainly responsible for raising the money to pay for the services it provides. But they also suggest that public leaders need to rethink the design of grants-in-aid. Grant programs can be restructured to promote productivity. In focusing attention on the fundamental links between service levels, cost, and grants design, Silkman and Young help us understand how to better make government do what we want it to do: provide the public services that citizens demand as efficiently as possible.

George E. Peterson, Director
Public Finance Center
The Urban Institute

PREFACE

It is an occupational hazard of publishing in the field of policy research that topics in vogue at the time a project is undertaken may be passe by the time a book reaches the marketplace, or interest may dissipate shortly after publication has taken place. One hears little nowadays, for example, about zero-based budgeting or large scale social experiments, though once such areas of inquiry were the hottest topics under the sun. Moreover, research on even more venerable subjects often quickly becomes outdated because analysis has used data that rapidly becomes obsolescent.

The present study, which analyzes the relationships between the financing of local government services through state grants-in-aid and the efficiency with which those services are produced, faces these same risks of obsolescence. Of necessity, analyses have been carried out on data from the mid-1970s that will lose currency as time goes on. Moreover, whatever special policy interests may have existed in the service areas of school bus transportation and public libraries which constitute the specific foci of these analyses, cannot be relied upon to persist or to attain wide attention in and of themselves. Nonetheless, having completed this study, we are struck by the increasing relevance of the basic questions and phenomena we have sought to investigate, and the possible answers to larger questions suggested by our analyses. The reasons for this perspective have to do with the growing attention to the two key elements in our study -- intergovernmental grants and concern over efficiency of public services -- in the policy deliberations that characterize the 1980s and perhaps the rest of the century. In addition, we believe we have touched upon certain fundamental elements of social science theory that are just now beginning to gain major attention by economists and organization scholars.

In order to elaborate our contentions of relevance it is useful first to review very briefly what exactly we have done in this book. First, we have tried to grapple seriously with the question of how to measure the efficiency of services that are not produced in the environment of the marketplace. Towards this end, we have offered an empirical strategy for estimating efficiency norms or "frontiers" associated with given levels of service output and showed how to explain deviations from these norms in terms of both quality variations and production inefficiency. More fundamentally, we have outlined a theory of why external financing, through grants-in-aid from a higher level of government to the level of government that actually delivers the service, is likely to affect the efficiency with which services are delivered. Here we specify both distortional effects stemming from alterations in the pricing of inputs to production, hence undermining efficient choices among those inputs, and motivational effects that lessen the incentives of local governments to minimize waste and corruption and maintain streamlined operations. The theory is confirmed by employing our empirical methodology to study, using independent sources of data, two very different services -- public libraries and school bus transportation. These are services for which states employ a wide variety of aid levels to assist provision by localities. Our results are highly consistent across these two very different service areas, and of a magnitude that indicates that public service inefficiencies can reach serious proportions and that financing through grants can affect the efficiency of local provision in a major way.

What then of the relevance of this research to future policy deliberations and research? There are at least three avenues worth noting. First, there is growing interest in certain major public service areas either to find ways to grapple with cost inflation, or to enhance service effectiveness, by reducing the hazards of third party financing. Second, there are theoretical questions in the areas of efficiency measurement and in organizational control that are just beginning to be explored by social scientists in a serious way. Third, and probably most significantly, the whole structure of federalism in the United States is undergoing revision, raising many important policy issues with respect to intergovernmental fiscal and organizational relationships and the efficiency of service production.

The two specific services chosen for study in this book -- libraries and school buses -- are certainly not the most socially significant from a present day policy point of view. Rather, these services were chosen for analytic simplicity and data availability. However, the theoretical foundations these case studies have enabled us to establish are relevant to a much wider set of services, some of which are presently undergoing significant scrutiny and debate. One such service is public schooling, a function which though locally delivered, commonly receives a major proportion of its funding from state government. The debates over school aid in the 1960s and 1970s focused largely on the question of equity, that is, How could school finance be made more fair by compensating for the unequal property tax bases of local school districts? More recently, however, concerns have turned more heavily to questions of efficiency and effectiveness, so that now the more commonly asked question is, How can the schools be made more effective in educating students for the competencies in reading, writing, mathematics, computers, and other skills they need to be properly prepared for the working world of the future or for higher education? Discussions have thus far centered mainly on teacher qualifications and pay levels, and concepts such as merit pay. Renewed attention has also been given to tax credits and vouchers as ways to introduce elements of competition into the school systems. Although there is an undercurrent of efficiency consciousness and awareness of comparative performance among schools, the issue of how properly to characterize efficiency remains to be adequately addressed. Moreover, and surprisingly, in view of the magnitude of expenditures involved, the connection of state aid to efficiency has not yet been raised to a high state of public consciousness. Districts do complain about lack of control over state-mandated services and concommitant budget requirements, but the full picture of both distortionary effects of state aid requirements and motivational losses that may inure from the fact that reductions in efficiency are financed largely by statewide rather than local taxpayers has not yet emerged. In view of the social significance of education, the concern about its effectiveness, and the magnitude of state aid in this arena, the joining of this debate would seem ultimately to be inevitable.

The service area in which the issues of financing and efficiency have been most explicitly raised is, of course, health care. Here the voluminous literature decries extant incentives for consumers and suppliers of health care to overspend on services and to be less than vigilant in monitoring the efficiency and propriety with which resources are used in this sector. As a result, major changes in the structure of health care financing are now being implemented or tested. Among these reforms are prescribed payment systems that limit suppliers in advance to prescribed budgets rather than provide retrospective reimbursement, and diagnostic-related group (DRG) systems that pay for patient care using fixed prices set in advance on the basis of initial diagnoses. These are obviously attempts to avoid the tendency of the conventional third party payment system (composed of both governmental aid programs and private insurance) to pay whatever the supplier chooses to prescribe and charge for, as allowed by the lack of consumer scrutiny or other forms of local control. Clearly the motivational effects with which we grapple here in the grants-in-aid context are at work in health care, and the concepts of copayments for insurance often recommended as a partial solution in health care reflect the same notion we stress -- that the more remote the financing, the less vigilant will be the consumer and the less accountable and efficient will be the producer.

The present effort also finds itself in the midst of some interesting cross-currents in the theoretical literature. In this study we have tried to advance the available methodology for estimating efficiency frontiers. This effort builds on Harvey Leibenstein's concept of X-efficiency, on work by Ross and Burkhead in measuring productivity in the public sector, and other contributions. The foregoing developments have, unfortunately, taken place in the backwater of economics because they challenge the general notion of highly rational, efficiency-seeking behavior upon which conventional economic theory is based. But the trend line for studying productive inefficiency is definitely rising as interest increases not only in the failings of private sector organizations, but in the inappropriateness if not irrelevance of assuming optimizing behavior in the nonmarket -- public and nonprofit -- sectors of the economy. Thus mathematical programming techniques such as data envelopment analysis, and various other ways of defining and measuring efficiency frontiers continue to hold a fascination and command increasing attention of analysts and method developers.

The present study also confronts certain issues of organizational control that are increasingly occupying the attentions of theorists. Known in the trade as "principal and agent theory," this avenue of inquiry seeks to ask what kinds of institutional arrangements best allow a group of clientele (or a funding body) to control the behavior of the agency that is contracted to actually carry out a given task. For example, is it best to shop for combinations of input services in the marketplace, or to integrate activities within a corporate structure that can directly utilize hierarchical command mechanisms? Viewed from a certain angle, the present study also grapples with this question. In particular, to what extent can a state which provides aid funds to localities, along with various auditing and regulatory controls, expect to have the localities use those funds efficiently for the designated purpose? What arguments can be applied to suggest that the state might be better advised to produce its services directly, or to the contrary, to turn both the financing and provision over to localities entirely? We believe that the present study has something to contribute to the search for answers to such questions. Certainly we have tried here to disabuse ourselves of the naive notion of earlier theoretical discussions of grant-in-aid systems, that states could expect to "optimize" public service provision simply by altering the financial parameters under which local governments operate.

The most dramatic recent development concerning intergovernmental grants and efficiency is, of course, the set of major changes encompassed under the new federalism promoted by the Reagan administration. Though many of these changes or proposals derived from shifts in relationships occurring throughout all levels of government in the 1970s they have come to a focus at the federal level in the early 1980s and represent a major turning point in American governance. In general, these reforms can be characterized by fiscal austerity through limits on taxation and spending; simplification of intergovernmental aid through consolidation of categorical programs into a few large block grants and through elimination of constraints and regulations such as matching requirements, reporting requirements, and minimum set-aside requirements for spending on particular programs; and a sorting out of functional responsibilities by levels of government, such as the proposed swapping of federal responsibility for Medicaid in exchange for state responsibility for AFDC and food stamps; and reduced dependence on grants-in-aid, at least from the federal government, to finance public services.

Though the present study has by itself no definitive judgments to offer with respect to these developments, the relevance of our discussion here is clear. Imposed limits on spending by government have heightened consciousness of the necessity for the public sector to produce more with less. If a good deal of what local and state governments do is essential to the welfare of their respective constituents, and if it now becomes difficult to rely on increased taxes or external aid to finance those services, then ways must be found to improve efficiency, first by trying to measure it more precisely, and then by devising production methods and incentives to bring governmental producing units, or their contractors, closely to identified norms of efficiency.

So too, simplification of grants-in-aid programs raises other, even more intriguing, issues alluded to in the present study. For example, will the elimination of reporting requirements by local or state agency grant recipients reduce efficiency by short-circuiting the ability of granting agencies to monitor and audit these recipients? Or, to the contrary, will the elimination of matching and categorical expenditure requirements increase efficiency by eliminating the costs of bureaucratic oversight? More fundamentally, might not such changes increase efficiency through enhanced local accountability brought on by the fact that simpler grant programs are easier for local citizens to understand and thus control, or because a dollar saved can now be more easily used to grant local tax relief?

Finally, will not the consolidation of financing and provision of a given public service within the same level of government tend to improve efficiency by eliminating the distortional effects of grants from one level of government to another, and by removing the motivational losses stemming from the incentives associated with spending other people's money? And even more provocatively, can reductions in the proportions of government spending financed by grants such as has taken place in the federal-state arena of the 1980s, be compensated by efficiency gains derived from the foregoing effects? Our study suggests that this may indeed be partly the case.

The aims of the present volume are very modest and cannot fully envelop the answers to the various major issues and questions associated with financing of major services, theory and measurement of organizational and public service efficiency, and implications of the new federalism. But the ideas and provocative empirical findings put forth here suggest a strong connection between our results and the pursuit of answers to these larger questions. In any case, it is comforting to feel that in carrying out this study we may have latched onto a train heading out into the future of policy research. For no longer can studies that refuse to presuppose optimizing behavior on the part of economic, bureaucratic, or political decisionmakers be summarily cast aside, only to rust on remote sidings.

Richard Silkman
Dennis Young
July, 1984

ACKNOWLEDGMENTS

This study would not have been possible without the help of many people who served in the capacities of advisors, outside supporters, consultants, and research staff.

The book emerges from studies over several years, supported by National Science Foundation grants numbers APR77-0910 and DAR-7824557. We wish to give special thanks to program officer Dr. Trudi Miller for the fairness and confidence she showed us during this period.

Very special thanks are due to our colleagues Professor Stephen J. Finch and Professor Gary Simon for the analytical assistance and insights they provided during the treacherous early and middle stages of the research.

The project benefitted greatly from feedback received from members of the project's external advisory committees. We wish to single out several people for special thanks including George Peterson, Malcolm Getz, Howard Chernick, Jerry Fastrup, G. Ross Stephens, Harvey Galper, James Jarrett, and David McKay. We also want to thank D. David Brandon, Susan Grasso, Sandy Frucher, Betsy Buechner, and Carol Schlageter-Chady for their staff and consultation efforts on behalf of the project.

The project was fortunate to involve a number of very talented and devoted graduate students including Tom Thibideau, Margery Grennon Bruno, Alayne Katz, Jacqueline Grennon, Sheryl Silverman, Ching-Mei Chang, Judy Manfredo, Augustus Olu-Hamilton, Mei-Ping Tang, James Gennaro, Jane-Marie Wright, Eileen Finkel, David Kohn, Noritaka Kobayakawa, Joseph Laia, and Birgit Noh.

Many people, all over the country and too numerous to mention, gave of their time and provided or guided us to sources of data and key information through telephone conversations and written correspondence. We thank them all.

Partial results of this study were published earlier in the National Tax Journal (September 1982) and in Perspectives on Local Finance and Public Policy edited by John Quigley, Jai Press (1983).

Finally, we apologize if we have inadvertently failed to mention other key contributors to this effort.

CONTENTS

GRIN and BEAR IT by FRED WAGNER

"The taxpayers spend millions of dollars to maintain this agency . . . It's only right that they should know how it's wasted."

1

THE CONTEXT OF GRANTS-IN-AID

> . . . delegating the power to spend without the responsibility for raising the money . . . is a recipe for run-away inflation in expenditure. . . .*
>
> Rudolf Klein, Professor of Social Policy
> University of Bath, England
> British Medical Journal
> February 9, 1980

THE FISCAL ENVIRONMENT

The system of paying for services through the auspices of "third-party" institutions has grown rapidly over the last three decades, and in a wide variety of circumstances. For example, with the growth of home ownership and automobile ridership, private property and liability insurance has become commonplace, and large insurance companies pay the bills for damages incurred in accidents, fires, crimes, and other situations. And health care, which used to be largely financed by direct fees from patients to doctors, or from patients to hospitals, now is overwhelmingly covered by private and governmental insurance and reimbursement programs. That cost inflction has rapidly accelerated in these areas of the economy is not unrelated to the growth of third party arrangements.

*Statement made in reference to a proposal to turn over control of local units of the National Health Service to local authorities while continuing to finance NHS centrally.

In particular, third party financing of hospital care has risen from about 50 percent in 1950 to approximately 90 percent today (Russell, 1977). At the same time, expenditures on medical care grew from less than 5 percent of GNP in 1955 to 8.6 percent in 1976 and has now reached 10.5 percent. Medical care expenditures are projected to be 15 percent of GNP by the year 2000. From 1950 to 1976 medical costs rose 2000 percent and hospital costs 1000 percent, compared to 125 percent for the consumer price index as a whole (Nielsen, 1979). Since 1976, medical costs have doubled again while costs for a hospital room have soared 230 percent (Statistical Abstract, p. 106). The Medicaid and Medicare programs instituted in 1966 are blamed for the major share of the inflationary spiral. From 1950 to 1965 cost per patient day in hospitals rose 7 to 8 percent annually. From 1965 to 1978, however, the comparable rate was 12 percent. In each period about half the rate of growth can be attributed to higher input prices and the other half to additional use of inputs (Russell, 1977). The diagnosis of the problem is suggested by Russell:

> The incentive structure created by high levels of third party payment is transforming medical care from a traditional market in which each patient and his doctor must weigh the possible benefits of care against its costs, to one in which they are able to act as if resources were free.

Government services are, of course, the generic case of third party payment. Government has always provided services to citizens, and picked up the tab indirectly, through taxation. Nonetheless, the third party payment phenomenon has become more intense and worrisome recently in the public sector as well. Two things have happened in the decades since the 1930s. Government has expanded the scope of services which it provides, and government has separated more and more, within its own federal structure, the function of service delivery from the function of service financing.

The first of these trends is widely known and appreciated. Between 1940 and 1982, for example, governmental expenditures increased from 14 percent to 36.1 percent of GNP, and accelerated rapidly in the 1950s and 1960s. Over this same period, the state and local government sectors grew from 8 percent to 15.8 percent of GNP. Since 1976, however, state and local government spending has leveled off, with spending increases falling behind the inflation rate (ACIR, 1981). Nonetheless, government expenditures now represent a much larger proportion of the U.S. economy than they did in the recent past.

To what extent the expenditure increases have resulted in the expansion of real output is uncertain, however. Sunley's (1976) analysis shows that for state and local governments over the 1962-72 period, only 13 percent of expenditure increases can be explained by increases in workload. Another 52 percent is explained by price increases. A residual category which Sunley calls "scope and quality" accounts for the rest. However, only the workload factor is certain to represent an increase in output. Price increases might reflect a better quality of inputs or just an increase in rents to factors of production (for example, higher salaries for the same employees). "Scope and quality" can by no means be unambiguously interpreted as such. Increases in slack, waste, corruption, or other manifestations of inefficiency are an equally valid interpretation as increases in quality or variety of services offered. In the empirical analyses we present later in the book, we are forced to face up to this problem of separating quality from inefficiency in order to measure and analyze the efficiency of local government services.

The main object of governmental expenditure increases has been spending for domestic social welfare purposes. Such spending, which includes social insurance, public assistance, health and medical programs, veteran's programs, education, housing, and other such functions, increased from $23.5 billion in 1950 to $493.3 billion in 1980 (ACIR, 1981). In percentage terms, these expenditures have risen from 8.9 percent of GNP in 1950 to 18.7 percent of GNP in 1980 and from 37.4 percent of total government expenditures in 1950 to 51.4 percent of such expenditures in 1980.

Much of the increase in social welfare spending has come from the federal government, so that over the 1950 to 1980 period, state and local expenditures have declined from 55.2 percent to 38.5 percent of all such government spending. This effect has been most dramatic for social insurance programs for which the state and local share has dropped from 57.5 percent in 1950 to 16.7 percent in 1980. By contrast, the corresponding numbers for education are 97.6 percent and 89.2 percent.

The latter figures are indicative of the fact that the aforementioned second trend -- a shift in fiscal responsibilities for government services from lower to higher levels of governments, and a concommitant disengagement of service financing from service delivery -- is just as drastic as the rate of government expenditure itself. Thus, the federal government has increased its share of the financing of many services delivered by state and local governments, and the states have assumed increased financial responsibilities for services previously paid for by local governments. To put this in perspective, state and federal intergovernmental grants each grew from around 1 percent of GNP in 1950 to 3.75 percent in 1981.

In terms of dollars, intergovernmental aid to local governments has grown from $6.4 billion in 1955 to $111.4 billion in 1981. Generally, federal aid has been the faster growing component, rising from 2.5 percent to 13.0 percent of own-source local revenues between 1955 and 1982 compared to 40.6 percent and 58.0 percent for state aid to local governments (ACIR, 1984). In 1962, federal and state aid amounted to 44 cents per dollar of own-source local general revenue. By 1982, this figure had risen to 71 cents (ACIR, 1984). Moreover, while general revenue for local governments grew at an annual pace of 12.5 percent over the 1967-72 period, revenues from own-sources grew by only 11.4 percent while federal and state aid grew by 21.2 percent and 15.3 percent, respectively. The same relative picture applies to the 1972-77 period where own-source revenues, growing at 9.4 percent, lagged the general revenue pace of 11.3 percent and the federal and state annual growth rates of 29.5 percent and 11.3 percent, respectively (ACIR, 1980). Between 1977 and 1981, the pace of growth has slowed, but the annual growth in revenues from own sources (6.1%) continued to lag that of federal aid to localities (7.3%) and state aid to local governments (12.1%). The result of these trends is that many services, which earlier were largely or exclusively local or local/state functions, are now paid for in significant proportions by the state and federal governments. In effect, the direct relationship between local taxpayers and local service recipients has been severed or severely weakened. Higher levels of government have become the third party payers for local government consumers.

In the private sector, some of the consequences of third party payment systems have become well known. The "moral hazard" associated with insurance systems has led to abuse and fraud in the filing of claims for damages of various kinds, and in the "overuse" of services for which no out-of-pocket payments are required. In the health area, the third party payment system is widely blamed for the fact that hospital and medical care lead the economy in the rate of cost inflation.

In general, the means through which third party payment causes these effects are fairly obvious. Consumers who face a zero price at the margin will consume higher and higher levels of services until the net marginal benefit of another unit of consumption falls to zero. And consumers who feel they will not be caught and/or punished for fraudulent claims will apply for higher reimbursements than they are entitled to since the costs reflected in higher premiums will be spread thinly over all insured parties. Moreover, consumers who are "being reimbursed anyway" have little incentive to check if their service suppliers have inflated their fees, made the "quality" of their services unnecessarily lavish, or charged for services that were not fully rendered.

For public services, however, recognition that third party phenomena have grown, and the manner in which these effects have been translated into serious problems, seem to be less well understood. After all, government has always financed its activities mainly through taxes, and while public sector expansion into service areas previously occupied by the private sector has been noticeable, it has not been overwhelming in the postwar United States. Until one begins to distinguish the implications of housing responsibilities in different parts of "the government" and one begins to get a grip on measuring the efficiency of resource use by government, the incremental changes due to third party effects are not so obvious. One goal of this book is to provide such a handle.

An exposition of the causal relationships which link grant-in-aid financing to losses in efficiency of local government services will be reserved for the next chapter. Suffice it to note at this point that local citizens may be expected to lose their incentives and abilities to hold government accountable for its services, as the costs of those services become more obfuscated by the remoteness of higher level governments and the complexity of intergovernmental relationships, and as the costs of local service usage becomes spread over all citizens within the jurisdiction of the higher level of government that has assumed the financing responsibilities. In Chapters 2 and 3 we describe a specific model through which these tendencies become manifest. For the present, however, it is useful to review in more detail the general character of the grant system itself as it has developed in the United States over the last 30 years.

CHARACTER OF GRANTS-IN-AID

The Magnitude and Scope of Grants-in-Aid

The U.S. grant-in-aid system has changed over time, both in the nature of services funded and in the structure of the grants themselves. At the federal level, emphasis has shifted away from agriculture, income security, and transportation towards community and regional development, education, training, employment and social services, general purpose fiscal assistance, and health over the 1957 to 1982 period. At the state level, education rose slightly as a percentage of state aid and highway aid diminished proportionately over the same period of time (Break, 1980). As of 1982, education aid absorbed 61.5 percent of state intergovernmental aid to local governments compared to 13.9 percent for public welfare, 14.8 percent for general revenue sharing, 5.1 percent for highways, and lesser percentages for other functions (ACIR, 1984). However, federal and state components differ substantially in their functional compositions, with state aid going more heavily to education (61.5% compared to 3.5%) and federal aid more oriented to housing (9.8% compared to less than 1%), public assistance (32.1% versus 13.9%), and other miscellaneous functions (State Government Finances, 1983).

It is also well to recognize the variations that exist in the use of state and federal aid among different types of local governments and among the 50 states. (The empirical analyses presented later in the book exploit the latter variation in order to discern the effects of different state aid levels.) The different types of local governments include counties, municipalities, townships, school districts, and other special districts. Dependence on intergovernmental aid varied from 29.1 percent of general revenues for townships to 53.4 percent for school districts in 1982 (ACIR, 1984). The corresponding numbers for counties and municipalities were 41.1 percent and 33.3 percent, respectively. Special districts (including some library districts which enter our empirical studies later in the book) depend on intergovernmental aid for 28.1 percent of their general revenues.

States also exhibit considerable variation in the degree with which their governments (state and local) depend upon intergovernmental revenues. For example, states ranged from a high of $686 per capita of intergovernmental aid in New York to a low of $141 per capita of such aid in New Hampshire, in 1976-77 (ACIR, 1980). The mean for all states was $308 with $196 of that representing net state aid, and the rest federal aid including that part which is passed through the state to local governments. States also range widely in the share of general expenditures financed by state and local governments from their own sources. States such as Kansas and Oklahoma finance 80 percent and 90 percent of their expenditures from their own sources, while states such as New Jersey and Wisconsin fall in the 50 percent to 60 percent range (ACIR, 1984). Still, it is clear that a great deal of variation exists in the extent to which local and state governments depend upon intergovernmental revenues to finance their expenditures on various services.

The Structure and Form of Grants-in-Aid

In recent years, grant instruments have shifted somewhat in structure and form from categorical grants tied to highly specific services and programs towards block grants, covering general categories of services, and towards general revenue sharing. For example, general purpose fiscal assistance which represented only 3 percent of federal grant funds in 1957 and only 2 percent in 1967 increased to 8.7 percent by 1978. (It has since fallen to 5.2% in 1982). Similarly, broad-based block grants for functional areas such as community development, health, criminal justice, social services, and employment training, increased from 8.4 percent to 14.7 percent of federal grant revenues between 1972 and 1978 (Break, 1980). The movement towards more generalized intergovernmental revenue flows is a continuing one, consistent with the Reagan administration's emphasis on the "new federalism" and decentralizing government authority. Still, unless the new federalism results in a massive dismantling of federal government programs and is widely adopted by the states, the bulk of intergovernmental revenues will remain categorical in nature (Peterson 1982, 1984). However, within this classification, there is considerable variation in the nature of formulas and other stipulations used to allocate funds and control their use, variations which may differentially affect how efficiently services are delivered.

State and federal categorical grant-in-aid programs vary on a number of key structural dimensions including the nature of the formula by which grant funds are distributed to localities, restrictions on the input factors and program technologies used by recipient local agencies, jurisdictional, organizational, and client eligibility requirements for program participation and other miscellaneous provisions.

In terms of their formal descriptions, grant-in-aid formulas generally fall into five categories: open-ended matching, closed-ended matching, lump sum appropriations, project grants, and shared taxes. The last of these -- shared taxes -- specify portions of a particular revenue source that are to be distributed to localities, as determined by formula. For example, state motor vehicle fees may be earmarked for distribution among localities according to some allocation formula. The size of the total distribution would depend upon the revenue stream in a given year.

For other types of grants, however, total program funds are fixed by appropriation in the state or federal budget and distributed to localities by some allocation formula. Under a project grant, for instance, the state allocates funds to localities on a project by project basis. Thus, a locality receives funds only after a proposed project is approved (for example, established screening standards are met) and its proposal is selected from among eligible candidates on the basis of relative merit or other (political) criteria. Project grants may have formula specifications (for example, they may require local matching funds), but they differ from other types of categorical grants in their project-specific nature and their lack of mandatory requirements for distributing funds to all eligible localities.

There are three variations of grants which are differentiated by the nature of the matching or reimbursement requirements between the funder and recipient levels of government, and the open- versus closed-end nature of fund availability. Under open-ended (matching) grants, a local jurisdiction receives a certain number of dollars for every dollar it spends of its own funds on a given program. The ratio of grant funds to own spending may be fixed, or may vary among localities by some additional formula factor, but there is no limit or ceiling on total funds that may be received by a locality under this arrangement. However, there is likely to be an appropriated limit for the state as a whole. In such cases, the effective matching or reimbursement rate is reduced below the statutory rate in order to accommodate projected usage. For example, a state may have a 90 percent reimbursement program on its books but only appropriate funds to allow 50 percent reimbursement.

Another open-ended grant scheme may be termed "unit price reimbursement." Here, funds are furnished to localities according to the number of units of service provided. Units of service may be of an output nature, for example, the number of children transported to school or the number of school lunches served, or of an input nature such as the number of route-miles or the number of personnel of a given type used to produce the service in question. The prices paid per such unit may be fixed or may vary among localities according to some additional formula factor.

Under closed-end matching grants, the recipient locality may receive matching or reimbursement funds in some prespecified ratio, up to some ceiling after which no further grant funds may be received. The ceiling may be based upon some allotment formula for distribution of a fixed total appropriation among localities.

Finally, in the case of lump sum grants, a fixed level of funds is allocated to each locality on the basis of some distribution formula and local matching funds are usually not required.

Grant formulas vary in the indexes they frequently use to allocate funds among alternative jurisdictions. Often these indexes are intended to reflect service needs or fiscal capacities of local jurisdictions. Localities' service needs are often gauged by measures of population; for example, the relative size of a locality's total population is a common measure. For grant programs designed to address the needs of particular subpopulations, the relative sizes of these "target groups" are often used as measures of need (for example, relative populations of school children, elderly, low income, and so on). Other physical measures of need such as highway miles for a highway repair or maintenance program, for example, may also be used to suit specific purposes. Per capita income is commonly used as the index of a locality's relative fiscal capacity. Another index, as in the case of education, is property value or wealth (per student or per capita). Such indexes are incorporated into grant programs either through allotment formulas (which set ceiling levels on closed-end matching grants, or determine lump sum grants) or through formulas to set matching ratios or reimbursement rates in open-ended grants.

In addition to the distribution mechanism, it is common for grant programs to differentiate their support of particular input factors or their reimbursement for methods or technologies used by local agencies to accomplish program purposes. For example, school bus aid formulas frequently reimburse local school districts for new bus expenditures at a different rate than for maintenance and operation costs of older buses. In a similar vein, foster care programs for dependent or neglected children generally impose restrictions on the types of treatments and institutional settings eligible for reimbursement, and may reimburse these treatments and settings at substantially different rates.

Grant programs often include specifications regarding eligibility requirements, though typically all relevant localities qualify for aid considerations. However, it is not unusual for grant programs to impose restrictions on the type of organization that may receive funds and deliver services. For example, many nursing care programs require that ultimate service providers be not-for-profit organizations, and various educational programs such as educational TV and high school equivalency programs are restricted to public school districts rather than a wider array of possible delivery agents. Finally, grant programs often contain other structural components, such as "save harmless" provisions -- a frequent accompaniment to revisions, modifications, or reformulations of grant program formulas. Such provisions protect existing benefit shares by assuring that, for some given time period, each recipient locality will not receive less money under the new formulation than under the present one.

POLICY OBJECTIVES AND RESEARCH

Given that grants-in-aid come in a variety of forms and have become an increasingly important part of the public economy over recent years, it is well to recognize that grant programs have been intended to serve a number of different policy purposes and objectives in the U.S. federal system. It follows from this that the research that has been carried out on the grants-in-aid system by economists and other social scientists has focused mainly on these articulated purposes. One consequence is that certain unintended or unanticipated effects -- most notably implications for productive efficiency -- have been virtually ignored.

As reviewed by Break (1980) and Gramlich (1981), the U.S. grants-in-aid system can be seen to address four principal problems in the federal system: externalities, vertical fiscal imbalances, horizontal fiscal disparities, and redistribution to low income groups. Externalities refer to the spillovers of benefits of public services across border lines of political jurisdictions. Essentially, it is theorized that local governments have a tendency to undersupply certain public goods and services because they fail to account for benefits received by constituents outside their jurisdictions. Grants from a higher level of government, by lowering the effective price of supplying units of service, are then designed to induce higher levels of local production. In this sense, grants are seen to "optimize" the local allocation of resources by inducing local governments to produce at a level closer to that where marginal benefits are just offset by marginal costs for the society as a whole. State grant systems are intended to compensate for interlocal externalities while federal grants are generally intended to offset interstate benefit spillovers.

Vertical fiscal imbalance refers to the fact that higher levels of government have certain advantages in raising revenues compared to lower levels of government. For example, federal and state governments can depend more heavily on income taxes than local governments because individual localities face greater difficulties in enforcement and in facing up to competitive tax pressures of neighboring jurisdictions. Moreover, because income and other taxes used by higher levels of government are perceived to be more progressive than local taxes, because such taxes also tend to be more lucrative, and because higher levels of government may simply be more cost-effective in the physical collection of revenues (through scale economies), the tendency is for higher levels of government to accumulate revenues at the expense of lower levels. On the other hand, lower levels of government are perceived as being more efficient on the expenditure and service delivery side, as they operate at a smaller and more manageable scale, closer to the citizenry. For this reason, and because of desires for tax progressivity and deconcentration of power of the central government, the grant system is intended to allow efficient central revenue collection, but also more efficient decentralized expenditure by state and local governments.

Horizontal fiscal disparity refers to the fact that local (or state) jurisdictions have different capacities with which to raise tax revenues. Thus, a wealthy jurisdiction can support a high level of service with a relatively low tax rate, while a poor jurisdiction must tax itself at a high rate in order to raise enough revenue for a moderate level of service. This issue is most salient in the area of public school financing where the courts have been active in striking down school financing systems that impose such differential burdens on local school districts. Grant-in-aid systems are sometimes designed to offset horizontal disparities by offering aid in reverse proportion to a locality's fiscal capacity.

Finally, grants are often said to address the needs of low income groups by subsidizing local government programs which offer services to these groups (for example, Medicaid and Aid to Families with Dependent Children) and by differentially allocating grant funds to poorer political jurisdictions.

Research on grants-in-aid has focused heavily on the externality issue, or more precisely on the degree to which grants succeed in inducing local recipient governments to actually spend more money for the subsidized services. In fact, this research, although voluminous, has been quite narrow in the sense that its focus has been expenditure behavior per se, and _not_ whether expenditure increases have led to proportionate increases of actual service output. (We shall have more to say about this later.)

More specifically, existing microeconomic literature on grants-in-aid has analyzed the price and income effects of grants, that is, how by changing both the effective local price of a given service and by increasing overall purchasing power available to recipient governments (relaxing their "budget constraints"), grants can induce those governments both to spend more on the subsidized service and to make substitutions between that service and other services or benefits (including local tax reduction). (See Gramlich, 1977, for a review.) The magnitudes of these effects vary by type of grant system. For example, lump sum grants are generally viewed to have a pure income effect, that is, to relieve the fiscal constraint on local governments without affecting the relative prices of different services. Matching grants, on the other hand, will in general result in both income and substitution effects. As summarized by Gramlich (1977), all types of grants are found to stimulate overall levels of recipient government spending, but the degree of such stimulation varies from the relatively elastic case of closed-end conditional (project) grants, to the less elastic case of open-ended matching grants, to the generally least elastic lump sum types of grants.

The foregoing conventional analyses of grant-in-aid implications for local government spending not only ignore the question of whether the increased expenditure is associated with greater physical output, but they rather assume that local governments behave as efficient utility-maximizing economic agents. One exception to this rule is the work of McGuire (1973) and others (for example, Courant, et al., 1979) on the so-called "flypaper effect." The latter suggests that some potential sources of local revenues are more encouraging of local government spending than others. For example, local politicians and officials are less reluctant to spend grant funds than to raise local taxes from an equivalent tax cut by the state or federal government. This effect not only confirms the tendency of grants to stimulate local government spending, but also indicates disharmony between local voters and local officials, and a proclivity on the latters' part to spend money in a manner at odds with voters' desires and under conditions of minimum voter scrutiny.

Other research suggesting a connection between grants-in-aid and inefficiency is rare, although several scholars have developed general microeconomic models of inefficient behavior by local government. Niskanen (1971), for example, has modeled the proclivity of bureaucrats to maximize their budgets, leading to allocative and possibly productive inefficiency and resulting in overspending relative to the social optimum. Rose-Ackerman (1978) analyzed political corruption and how public officials tend to trade-off personal utility and reelection probabilities. And Wagner (1976) and others have analyzed the phenomenon of "fiscal illusion" under which local citizens are seen to underestimate the tax-price of local government services and hence authorize spending and service levels that are too high. In a more general sense, the works of Leibenstein (1966) on X-efficiency, March and Simon (1958) and Cyert and March (1963) on organizational slack, and Williamson (1964) on managerial discretion, all suggest that economic organizations (private or public) are prone to inefficiency, but none of these veins in the literature makes a direct connection with grants-in-aid. Break (1980) does, however, explain the connection between the flypaper effect and losses of productive efficiency within local governments. In addition, Break recognizes the potential inefficiencies associated with those grants that distort resource prices by differentially subsidizing inputs to production. (We shall call these "distortion effects" and elaborate upon them later.)

By and large, however, the possibility that intergovernmental grants introduce productive inefficiency into the provision of public services has been an unexplored domain. It is the purpose of the ensuing chapters to chart some of this territory.

2

THEORY AND CONCEPTS OF EFFICIENCY AND GRANTS-IN-AID EFFECTS

The foundations of the current system of grants-in-aid to state and local governments were laid down in an era when people believed that economic resources ought to be shifted more heavily to the public sector and that government was the appropriate and most efficient agent for addressing outstanding social needs. The most rapid growth of the intergovernmental revenue system was set into motion in the mid 1960s when the federal government undertook its War on Poverty and many social welfare programs were enacted. But the climate for government spending began to change in the early 1970s as concerns over the efficacy and efficiency of government as a service provider gathered momentum. As the costs of doing business in the public sector increased, tax limitation movements arose, beginning with Proposition 13 in California and including Proposition 2 1/2 in Massachusetts, among others. And as waste and corruption were exposed in various areas, such as Medicaid and Welfare, a number of specialized and general commissions were formed, nationally and within states, to address the problems of productivity and efficiency in government.

Ultimately some recognition has emerged that the intergovernmental revenue system may have something to do with the perceived problems of governmental efficiency. On an ad hoc basis, for example, states have begun to tie state formula grants to the efficiency of service delivery by localities. (See Buechner and Schlageter-Chady, 1981.) For example, various states adjust reimbursements for Welfare and Medicaid programs based on rates of error in benefit payments and client eligibility. Other productivity incentive provisions have also been tried or proposed by a number of states for higher education, elementary and secondary education, local transit, and other functions.

Unfortunately, efforts of the productivity commissions as well as the pragmatic attempts of states to insert productivity clauses into their aid programs have run up against some of the very tough conceptual and practical problems of defining and measuring efficiency and other aspects of service delivery performance. These very same problems must be addressed before one can effectively carry out research on the implications of grant-in-aid systems for governmental efficiency. Thus, we begin this chapter with a discussion of efficiency and productivity measurement in the public sector, before proceeding to consider precisely why we should expect intergovernmental grant programs to affect governmental efficiency at the local level.

EFFICIENCY DEFINED

Several interrelated terms are commonly used to consider questions of public program performance. These include efficiency, effectiveness, costs, quality, output, and productivity. Meanings attributed to these terms in the literature and in practice are often inconsistent and sometimes ambiguous. One of the better analyses of productivity in local government is that presented by Ross and Burkhead (1974). That study builds on the experience of productivity measurement in the private sector, and differentiates between inputs, direct outputs, consequences, and quality of goods and services, in developing its definitions and concepts. Following Ross's and Burkhead's lead, we can employ the following definitions:

Inputs are the labor, capital, and other resources used in the production of a service or good.

Costs are the values of these resources as measured by (competitive) market prices or opportunity values.

Direct Outputs are the immediate products of a service or program such as the number of police patrols or the number of student hours of instruction, or the number of students transported to school (see Chapter 5). In the private sector, the common denominator of dollars of "value added" is used to make comparisons across the variety of private goods and services. However, in the public sector this practice is usually precluded by the absence of market prices for services.

Consequences are the impacts of service outputs on the ultimate goals or purposes of the service program in question. For example, educational achievement or lower crime rates are the (intended) consequences of educational and police programs, respectively. (As discussed in Chapter 4, book circulation is such a quantity for public libraries.) Unlike direct outputs, however, consequences are not fully determined by decisions made internally by the agency administering a program, but are also partly determined by environmental variables such as socio-economic conditions.

Quality refers to certain characteristics of program outputs which affect service desirability, such as the tastiness of school lunches, the congestion experienced in travel, or the necessity of bringing garbage cans to curbside for pickup. Another aspect is the scope of services such as the provision of joint products. For example, libraries may provide reference assistance as well as book lending. The importance of quality in productivity considerations is that service outputs can be properly compared over time or among alternative producers only if these outputs are "homogeneous" with respect to quality.

Using these definitions, we can proceed to define efficiency, effectiveness, and productivity:

Efficiency is the direct output per unit cost, or the cost per unit of direct output, for a service or good of given quality.

Effectiveness is the degree of achievement of program consequences (objectives) which may be expressed in various ways including ratios of consequences to inputs (for example, test scores to teachers per pupil), consequences to outputs (e.g., test scores to hours of instruction), and consequences to pre-set goal targets (e.g., test scores compared to some test norm).

In the framework of Ross and Burkhead, productivity is basically an efficiency concept which is concerned with the efficacy of the production process through which a program produces its direct output. This is in contrast to concerns about how much impact such output has on ultimate service goals. Nor is productivity conceived to pertain to the question of whether the intended goals or direct outputs are appropriate in the sense of social preferences. Productivity is also conceived as a relative concept which requires appropriate comparisons, either over time or across alternative producers of a given product. In this context, we can conceive of various types of productivity improvements:

- an increase in direct output for given unit cost and quality levels
- an increase in quality for given cost and output levels
- a decrease in cost, at constant output and quality

It is also possible to consider changes in the productivity of specific input factors such as labor (for example, output per man-hour) as long as it is understood that improvements in such indexes may be due to a variety of sources including harder working personnel, better qualified personnel, better management, or higher capital-labor ratios. However, we will only be concerned here with overall or "total factor" productivity.

While the foregoing narrow definition of (total factor) productivity fails to deal with program effectiveness, it has a number of compensating advantages for purposes of the present study:

- We can avoid the analytical quicksand of trying to separate program impacts from the effects of environmental variables.
- We can circumvent (often irresolvable) discussions of what service goals out to be (for example, are the state universities producing too many graduates with advanced degrees?).
- We can sidestep discussion of "unwritten agendas" for service programs, such as having government serve as an "employer of last resort," or as a stimulant to the construction industry. (However, by first focusing on direct outputs per unit of inputs we might later try to explain apparently low productivity in terms of such ancillary objectives.)

While effectiveness questions are very important, there is more than enough area for valuable contribution to be made to the analysis of grant-in-aid effects by focusing on direct outputs. Furthermore, even with this simplification, questions of productivity analysis in the public sector are by no means without serious additional conceptual and empirical problems.

CONCEPTUAL PROBLEMS

Studying productivity incentives of grants-in-aid involves a number of serious analytical problems. The first of these is simply the fact that characterization of productivity requires the definition and measurement of output of the public service under scrutiny. Yet the measurement of public service outputs has long been a bugaboo both in conceptual terms -- What is the appropriate measure of output? -- and in practical terms -- Is the data available to measure it?

Unlike services in the private sector, measurement of output for public services in hindered by the lack of tangible output units such as loaves of bread or numbers of television sets. A unit of service output is transient and disappears immediately subsequent to its delivery. Thus, careful records must be kept to tally output, and inventories cannot be referenced as a check on such records. Furthermore, many public services admit to alternative possible output specifications. For example, is the output of police service the number of patrol car miles, the number of foot patrols, or the number of interventions or interrogations? These multiple possibilities stem from the fact that a given service may involve several functions, such as patrolling and investigation, and these functions may be performed in various ways (for example, foot versus patrol cars).

One severe problem in the public sector is that the variety in types and qualities of services cannot be "normalized" through the use of market prices to compute, aggregate, and compare the values of alternate outputs. No such market values exist, and the methods traditionally used by economists to gauge public sector output are essentially useless for productivity studies. For example, GNP computations use public sector expenditures to represent public sector outputs. By this definition, there can be no changes in productivity in this sector since expenditures would appear as both the numerator and the denominator of the ratio of output to cost. Another indicator of public sector output which has been used by economists in so-called determinant studies of governmental expenditure is the number of governmental employees. Here again the use of inputs as output indicators defeats the purposes of productivity analysis. The absence of a direct dollar-valued output measure for public services precludes comparison across services which vary by quality and type, while indirect public sector output measurement based on inputs precludes meaningful productivity measurement. Thus, it becomes necessary to attempt to obtain direct (nonmonetary) measures of output for individual types of public services and to try to correct for variations in quality in order to make productivity comparisons within given service types.

Unfortunately, output measurement in the public sector is still in a primitive state. The 1974 assessment of Ross and Burkhead still applies:

> There is very little information available on the direct outputs of local governments. Most local governments simply do not keep the data necessary to measure such outputs, and those that do have only recently begun to keep the data on a systematic basis. An Urban Institute survey of thirty cities and counties found that only about half of those surveyed collected cost data by activity and program on a routine basis, about three-fourths collected workload information, slightly less than one-third collected data on cost per unit workload and only four -- Chicago, Dade County, Dayton, and Los Angeles -- regularly collected effectiveness or impact data. Even in those few jurisdictions where the necessary data are available, because of the fragmentation of local governments and differing patterns in the assignment of responsibilities, much of it is not comparable among jurisdictions.

Further problems emanate from the difficulty of measuring quality differences and in correcting for those differences. As for outputs, it often seems necessary to gauge quality in terms of inputs. Numbers of staff per client is a favorite proxy for quality, for example. An obvious difficulty here, however, is that quality or efficiency improvements that might result in more effective use of staff, or the substitution of other inputs for labor, would be recorded as a decline in quality.

Another concern is the measurement of costs. Funds expended by the state and matched by the locality may be clearly defined, but the real resources devoted to a program might be less obvious. Overhead expenses must be properly allocated and care must be taken that items devoted to program use, but not included in the administering agency's budget (for example, centrally administered supplies) are included in a consistent way across jurisdictions and/or over time. External costs imposed by local programs also do not appear in budgets, but should be accounted for. For example, an undermaintained bus system may look cheap in a budget statement but may impose pollution and injury costs on riders and other citizens. (Note that these concerns plague private sector productivity measurement as well.) An additional set of problems emanates from the fact that localities vary in the size of their programs and the nature of their clientele. Often there will be cost variations associated with these factors because of economies of scale, start up or one time costs, or varying needs of different clients. Productivity analysis must control for these factors if fair comparisons are to be made among different types of jurisdictions.

Despite these various difficulties, progress is discernible for productivity measurement in the public sector in recent years. For example, Ross and Burkhead (1974) and others have been able to adapt to the limitations of output and quality measurement and the variety of public sector outputs by statistically separating observed changes in public sector expenditures into components attributable to changes in workload (for example, clients served), changes in unit costs of inputs, and a "residual" which may crudely be further dissected (statistically) into quality and productivity components. In this approach, outputs are approximated by workload, unit input costs are approximated by an index such as starting salaries, quality is approximated by various ad hoc (input related) indicators, and productivity improvement is calculated as the unexplained remainder. This approach has been used on a time series basis for relatively aggregated classes of public service categories such as welfare and education. Categorical grant programs, on the other hand, tend to be individualized to a more specific program component level and require analysis on a cross-section rather than time series basis across states and localities.

A final difficulty in studying productivity incentive effects in government has to do with the question of what constitutes an "incentive." The existence of an incentive to save money or use resources presupposes a basic motivation on the part of the recipient agency to keep its costs to a minimum or to improve quality and effectiveness. Cost minimization, for example, may be a fairly good assumption about individual citizens or profit-making firms, but it may be a precarious assumption about governments. To the contrary, some scholars have concluded that the bureaucratic and political motivations operate in the direction of wasting money rather than saving it. Or at best, government officials may be neutral in their concerns about efficiency and productivity. Thus, faced with opportunities to become more productive (through formula incentives) local government officials may choose not to take advantage. On the other hand, disincentives toward improved productivity may either be ignored or exploited.

In any case, a proper model of government behavior is needed to identify what constitutes an incentive and what does not. Opportunities to save money or to produce more output from a given allocation of resources constitute incentives only if government officials perceive that such accomplishments will be personally rewarding in some way. On the other hand, implicit incentives toward waste presuppose certain contrary objectives or insensitivity towards efficiency by government officials. The same applies to local citizens who are responsible for electing officials and keeping them accountable.

In the remainder of this chapter we shall identify the determinants of local government inefficiency which can be influenced by grants-in-aid to local government. In so doing, we must consider the question of behavior of participants in the processes of local government -- principally citizens, local public officials, and (secondarily) state administrators.

THEORY OF GRANTS AND PRODUCTIVITY

In the introductory chapter we broadly suggested that grants cause inefficiency in local governments through the consequences of "third party financing" which was seen to give consumers the "wrong" price information and inadequate incentives to scrutinize the behavior of service suppliers. Actually, this general hypothesis entails a number of different but intertwined strands. Below, we shall identify these strands and elaborate upon their operation. In the next chapter, we focus on the most important elements identified here for the purpose of formulating a mathematical model of grant-related efficiency behavior, which will be estimated empirically thereafter.

Broadly speaking, we hypothesize that grants-in-aid may have four different but interactive types of efficiency-related effects on recipient governments. We call these "distortion" effects, "incentive" effects, "information" effects, and "supervision" effects.

Distortion effects

The concept of distortion is based on a simple principle of microeconomic theory. Grants, by altering the prices faced by local governments so that these prices no longer reflect true resource costs, may lead local governments to select inefficient input combinations or to choose inefficient production strategies. Grant-in-aid formulas frequently do alter the relative prices of inputs and/or intermediate outputs faced by localities. By changing effective local prices, a grant formula may induce local agencies to switch to production techniques that are more intensive in the now cheaper input or to alter output mix in favor of the more highly reimbursed intermediate output.

This effect is illustrated in Figure 2.1. The horizontal axis represents input(s), X_2 to production that are subsidized by the grant program (for example, personnel), while the vertical axis represents the unsubsidized input(s), X_1 (e.g., equipment). The unsubsidized prices of these inputs are P_2 and P_1, respectively. The budget line B represents the resources which the locality would devote to the service in the absence of the grant program, and Y represents service output. In the presence of the grant-in-aid formula which subsidizes input(s) X_2 by reimbursing a proportion m of total dollars with state dollars, the effective price of X_2 to the locality becomes P_2 (1-m). Thus, in these circumstances, the locality operates under an effective budget constraint B_1 and, if it is (locally) efficient, produces output level Y_1 at operating point Q_1.

It is clear from this diagram, however, that the grant structure can induce overall inefficiency. In particular, assume that the total expenditure at operating point Q_1 is B*. If a budget of B* were available at the original prices, then a higher level of output, Y_2, could be produced with the same total resources. (See operating point Q_2 on budget line B* in the diagram.) Thus, as long as P_1 and P_2 accurately reflect the real resource costs of X_1 and X_2, the differential subsidy structure of the grant will promote inefficiency.

Figure 2.1 can also be used to consider the case of grant programs which differentiate their funding of alternative program strategies. The classical cases involve preventative versus therapeutic or custodial services in child care, mental health, and other social and health areas. If we interpret X and X_2 as alternate intermediate outputs such as care days versus the number of preventative community treatments performed, respectively, and if Y is interpreted as a higher level output such as reductions in pathological cases, then it is clear that a program which differentially funds one strategy versus another will promote inefficiency.

FIGURE 2.1
Distortion Effects of a Differential Input or Intermediate Output Subsidy

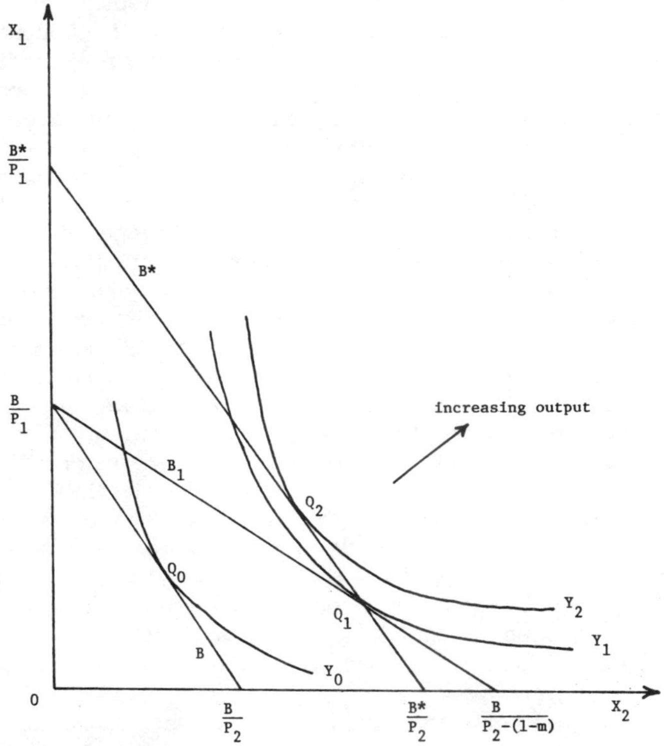

There are a number of other aspects of grant-in-aid programs that might be considered distortional in nature as well. Particular organizational auspices may be required by the state such as the use of not-for-profit contractors, although this may not be the most efficient strategy in every locality. Standards may be imposed with respect to personnel credentials, physical facilities and equipment, staff to client ratios, reporting requirements, and scale of operations, although these standards may not fit the needs of individual local jurisdictions very well. In such cases, localities may be induced by the availability of grant funds to use relatively inefficient operational policies, leading to higher overall costs. (A rather dramatic example of this was reported recently in the New York Times (Chira, 1982). It seems that Putnam County, New York wanted to widen a bridge to 21 feet at a cost of $240,000. However, in order to secure federal aid for this project, the county would have to widen the bridge to a 44 foot standard, at a cost of $640,000, although the local share would be only $31,200).

Even if grants are not discriminatory in their treatments of different inputs, production strategies, or intermediate outputs, we must still expect such aid to undermine the efficiency of local public services, because grants tend to loosen the reins of accountability which local citizens hold over local public officials. They do this through a combination of "information" and "incentive" effects that result from the fact that grants decrease the share of service revenues derived from local sources. Both these effects are based on the assumption that without effective oversight and supervision by local citizens, local public officials will tend to lose sight of efficiency considerations and allow their operations to become slack or engage in expenditure practices that harm productivity. Such an assumption is not difficult to justify. As a general principle, any organization can be expected to decline in its performance if not kept sufficiently in check by outside pressures. This is the central hypothesis behind Hirschman's (1970) analysis of "exit and voice," for example, and is consistent with the works of Cyert and March (1963) and others on the concept of organizational slack. Moreover, one can readily think of various considerations that might lead local politicians and bureaucratic officials to actively pursue objectives in conflict with the goal of local service efficiency. Niskanan's (1971) work, for example, is based on the contention that bureaucratic officials try to maximize their budgets because in doing so various benefits such as prestige, power, salary, and perquisites, are maximized too. Budget maximization, Niskanen shows, is often not consistent with productive efficiency.

Local elected officials also are subject to considerations which may induce them to make decisions or use their influence in ways that will cause local government operations to depart from productive efficiency. For example, Rose-Ackerman (1978) characterizes politicians' concerns in terms of two central factors -- personal income and votes (the probability of reelection). Each of these considerations can be seen to lead to behavior at variance with productive efficiency. For example, politicians may "buy" votes by catering to special interests through preferential contracts for supplies of services from particular contractors, or by excessive patronage appointments, and so on. Personal wealth may be enhanced through kickbacks and personal use of public resources. Such practices, whether blatant or the cumulative effects of small deviations of this kind, obviously detract from efficiency by using inputs of inferior quality or inflated prices, by employing more of given types of inputs (for example, employees) than is actually necessary to produce a given level of service output, or by diverting resources to unofficial uses. Nor is it necessary to invoke explicit or criminal mischief to support the assertion that politicians may be so diverted from putting resources to their most efficient use. The nature of the job, and the intrinsic concerns of politicians for political survival and personal well-being, would appear to exert a subtle influence of this kind, even on the well-intentioned. Thus, the viability of mechanisms of public accountability through citizen involvement and oversight, are crucial to keeping productive efficiency within reasonable bounds.

Unfortunately, grants-in-aid may be expected to undermine such accountability in the following ways:

Incentive effects

An increase in intergovernmental aid received for the production of a service will lower the direct fiscal effort required of local citizens to provide a given level of services, and will decrease the proportion of service expenditures financed locally. This, in turn, will reduce the financial incentive of local citizens to keep their local governments operating efficiently. The reason is that as the local share of revenues decreases, any savings in efficiency accrue more and more to taxpayers statewide (or nationwide), rather than to local taxpayers. Since the local share of state or national tax savings is normally very small, local taxpayers have little financial incentive to ensure local efficiency. Similarly, any losses due to a decline in local efficiency would be financed more and more by nonlocal taxpayers, as the local share of revenues decreases. That is, these taxpayers would foot more and more of the bill for local waste. The loss of incentive by local citizens to hold their local officials accountable for service efficiency may be expected to lead to greater laxity and more discretionary expenditure behavior by these officials, and hence to losses in the efficiency with which services are delivered.

Information effects

A second effect of grants-in-aid which operates in parallel with the incentive problem has to do with the <u>ability</u> of local citizens to hold their governments accountable. Essentially, as grants replace local revenue sources, local revenue and expenditure patterns become complicated and more obscure to local citizens. Under a grant arrangement, service revenues emanate from two or more sources, some of which local citizens may not even be aware. It then becomes more difficult for those citizens to know exactly what is being spent and for what purposes. Thus, citizens have a more difficult task monitoring the receipt and expenditure of funds by local officials even if they are motivated to do so. The result may again be a loss of effective accountability for local officials, allowing greater laxity and discretion, and leading to lower efficiency in service production.

Supervision effects

Distortion, incentive, and information effects all operate in the direction of reducing local governmental efficiency as grants-in-aid become a greater part of the financing of local services. There are certain compensating factors, however, which may mitigate these effects or conceivably even neutralize or overwhelm them. There are at least three kinds of possibilities here. First, grant programs inevitably cause local programs to grow, at least in budgetary terms. This makes the programs more visible relative to other programs, conceivably inviting greater scrutiny by local citizens.

Second, it is possible that some of the regulations and guidelines attached to grant programs actually reflect expert knowledge about the most efficacious strategies or methods of service delivery. Thus, inexpert localities may be guided towards more efficient operations through grant program participation.

Third, we may reasonably surmise that state (or federal) agencies responsible for disbursing and administering grant programs would be inclined to look over the shoulders of local program officials, and through audits, evaluations, and performance monitoring, influence local operations towards greater efficiency.

However, auditing activities normally focus on the propriety of expenditures on particular items, or on the following of mandated procedures, rather than on service efficiency per se, while evaluations are usually undertaken warily and at intervals too infrequent to control program operations. Thus, it is our overall expectation that the aforementioned potentially positive influences of grant programs on local government efficiency will not be as strong as the combined effects of distortion, incentive, and informational problems.

This is a matter for empirical verification, however. Furthermore, given that our expectations hold true, the idea of improved supervisory mechanisms may help compensate for productivity losses associated with grants-in-aid and may ultimately prove to be useful in attempting to synthesize policy alternatives to address the efficiency problems of intergovernmental aid. In particular, it is our impression that state evaluation, monitoring, and auditing practices are still in a rather primitive state, and that with some improvement and redesign might make a stronger contribution to the maintenance of efficiency of local government grant recipients.

PERSPECTIVE

In the next chapter, we formulate a mathematical model and empirical strategy for estimating the effects of grants-in-aid on local government efficiency. Despite the numerous variations and subtleties of alternative grant programs, we are forced by the data and modeling considerations to characterize grant programs very simply in terms of the proportions of expenditures financed locally versus externally. Within this framework, we test the basic hypothesis that as dependence on grants-in-aid increases, local government productivity is reduced through the combination of distortion, incentive, and informational effects. (A "negative" finding would, of course, provide impetus for the alternative interpretation that supervisory effects overwhelm these latter effects.) However, before we reach the point of estimating this relationship, we must develop an effective strategy for measuring inefficiency, taking into account the problems of output measurement and quality discussed earlier in this chapter.

3

METHODS AND MODELS

In this chapter, the theoretical concepts discussed in Chapter 2 are translated into mathematical models and methods for empirical estimation of the hypothesized effects. There are three central issues to be addressed. These are: (1) the measurement of inefficiency; (2) the determination of how inefficiency is manifested in terms of expenditures on alternative inputs to production; and (3) analysis of the causal determinants of inefficiency including the role of grants-in-aid.

MEASURING INEFFICIENCY

Operating inefficiency is fundamentally a relative concept. Pragmatically, an organization may be judged efficient or inefficient only in relation to other organizations producing similar outputs under similar operating conditions. While there may be a theoretically ideal process for producing a given quality of service at minimum cost, only actual production operations are ever observed. This state of affairs poses a certain difficulty for empirical research on productivity, for if we are to understand the determinants and manifestations of inefficiency, we must first know how much inefficiency there is. This necessitates the characterization of efficient production norms against which observed behavior can be compared.

The estimation of efficiency norms or production frontiers does not originate with us. Indeed, as the realization of the importance of inefficiency within organizations has grown among economists in recent years, a small but interesting literature has developed on the subject (for example, Huang and Crosswhite, 1979). The basic idea is to measure the performance of those organizations of a given type which appear to be the most efficient, and then to estimate the feasible limits of efficiency based on those observations. We note here that our concern is with both "technical" and "price" efficiency, to borrow the terms developed by Farrell (1957). Local government service producers can be inefficient either as a result of not fully optimizing within a given choice of technology (technical inefficiency) or as a result of choosing suboptimal technologies, given input prices (price inefficiency). Unfortunately, as we will point out in our empirical analyses later, the data do not permit the disaggregation of these two sources of inefficiency. Our approach as described below, should be contrasted with a recent development in mathematical programming -- "data envelopment analysis" (Charnes, Cooper, and Rhodes, 1978 and 1981), which focuses entirely on computing the technical inefficiency of local public service producers (or "decision making units," in their terminology). (See Sexton, Silkman, and Hogan, 1984).

Our approach of efficiency measurement proceeds as follows. Consider Figure 3.1 in which are plotted the outputs and total expenditures of a number of hypothetical local government agencies all of which produce similar outputs under similar production conditions. We define the lower bound envelope of such points as being a "quasi-minimum total cost" frontier (QMTC) in that it approximates the minimum costs required to produce each level of agency output. D_i is then defined as the ith agency's "deviation" from the QMTC frontier.

FIGURE 3.1
Graphical Representation of the QMTC Frontier
and Deviations from this Frontier

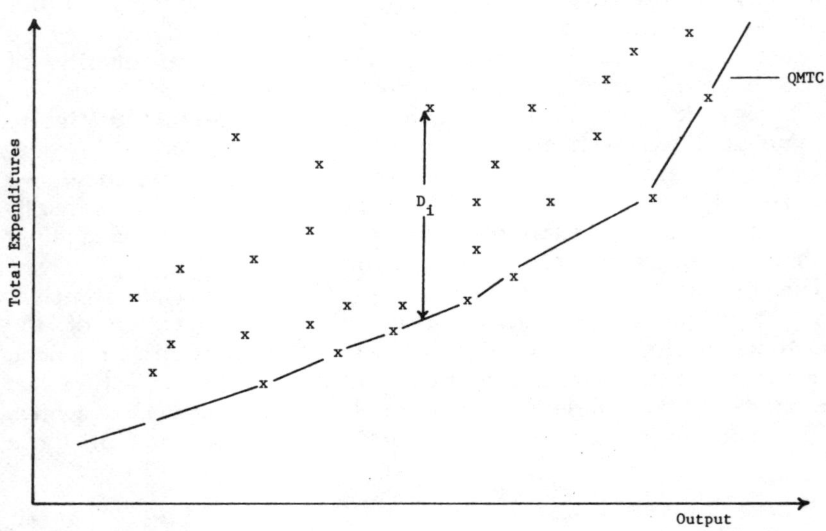

As a practical matter, construction of a QMTC frontier involves three important steps. First, an output measure must be identified for the service under scrutiny. This requires that services be selected for which a simple, quantifiable, and documented output index adequately captures service output. In the results presented in Chapters 4 and 5, we use the number of students transported to school as the output measure of pupil transportation programs, and the number of volume-hours made available to the public as the measure of output for public libraries.

The second step is to plot a scattergram of total operating expenditures versus output for a sample of local government service producers, such as that illustrated in Figure 3.1. The third step is statistically to estimate the lower bound envelope of points in the scattergram. This is carried out in Chapters 4 and 5 by taking logarithmic transformations of total expenditures and output, which linearizes the relationship between these variables, and then regressing one against the other. Subsequently, two estimated standard deviations are subtracted from the regression line to derive the frontier. This leaves some 2.5 percent of observations actually below the frontier, but yields a reasonable estimate of <u>achievable</u> efficiency for each level of output, as the appropriate criterion with which to characterize the efficiency levels of individual localities.

The obvious temptation is to characterize those agencies near the frontier as being efficient and those far above the frontier as being inefficient. Unfortunately, output of public agencies is rarely standard and almost never of identical quality or produced under identical conditions. Thus, deviations may represent higher costs associated with different production conditions over which the agency has no control (for example, population density, local price levels, and so on), or joint products or better quality services. Moreover, the quality issue has to be scrutinized very carefully. In particular, it is important to distinguish between quality increments which have been demanded by local citizens (which we call "demanded quality") and quality increments that have been "perpetrated" by local officials as a matter of their own indulgences. For example, adding staff to a school or library or social agency may improve the nominal quality of services rendered, but if local voters would rather not have spent the money that way such an increment should actually be classified as inefficiency.

Despite these complications, the efficiency frontier concept has intuitive appeal since the deviations measure differences in costs of production between an agency and a sister agency producing nominally similar levels of services. That the QMTC frontier is determined by actual and not hypothetical agency operations supports its feasibility and use as an efficiency benchmark. The trick is to correct for, through modeling, whatever variations obtain in quality and production conditions so that actual inefficiency levels can be compared. In this spirit, deviations from the QMTC frontier are usefully analyzed in two respects: (1) to find out where the "extra" expenditures are going, that is, what kinds of items (for example, personnel, equipment) they are expended on, and (2) whether the deviations are caused by demands for higher service quality, production condition differences, or inefficiencies.

To address the first issue, we employ what we term a "sink analysis." The second question is addressed by means of a "determinant analysis."

SINK ANALYSIS

This mode of analysis is based on the simple accounting principle that dollars spent must fall into one of three general categories or "sinks" -- labor costs, nonlabor operating costs, and capital costs. Essentially, the sink analysis proceeds by examining individual agency expenditure patterns and correlating them with the magnitude of the deviations of those agencies. As a second step, the deviations are regressed against the individual sinks to determine at the margin whether or not the expenditure categories differentially contribute to higher total expenditures. While the sink analysis alone can neither identify the magnitude of operating inefficiency nor its determinants, it provides useful insights into the nature of higher expenditures.

For example, the analysis will reveal how much variation there actually is in expenditure patterns among localities. Wide variations in spending among the three categories of inputs would suggest, though not prove, the presence of reasonably large numbers of localities using suboptimal input combinations or production techniques. A low variance, on the other hand, would suggest that most agencies use roughly the same (presumably efficient) production methods. Analysis at the margins can be even more revealing as it indicates which inputs are overused relative to others. For example, such analysis may reveal whether a dollar spent at the margin for additional personnel contributes more to inefficiency and less to output than say a dollar on supplies or equipment. Such a finding would suggest roughly how inefficiency is manifested in terms of actual expenditure behavior, and may indicate the forms which organizational slack and discretionary expenditure behavior by public officials appear to take.

In principle, a sink analysis can be pushed to the point of separating the sources of inefficient spending on particular inputs into price and quantity effects. For example, if the marginal contribution to inefficiency of expenditures on labor is high, is this because the wages paid to employees are too high, or because too many employees are hired? Unfortunately, however, the precision of accessible data precludes exploiting a sink analysis to this degree, at least for the services available for analysis in Chapters 4 and 5.

DETERMINANT ANALYSIS

In this mode of analysis, we attempt to answer why productive inefficiency occurs, and in particular, whether state aid is a causal factor. More generally, in the framework of our model, we seek to explain deviations from the QMTC frontier in terms of demand for quality, local production conditions, and the magnitude of state aid.

On the demand side, we postulate that local constituents recognize a tax-price, t, associated with improvements in the quality of services provided by the local agency. We argue that t should reflect <u>local</u> tax rates only, and not any direct local contributions to state aid. This is justified for two reasons: First, voters are generally poorly aware of the fiscal relationships that characterize revenue and expenditure flows at the state level, and hence may ignore or be unaware of state aid. Second, a local community's use of state aid normally represents a small proportion of overall state aid. Thus, any increases in state taxes due to a given community's use of aid are spread thinly over the entire state. Even if constituents were perfectly aware of the local consequences of state taxes and expenditures, they would view state aid as a public good, the local use of which is essentially costless. Accordingly, demanded quality (per capita, above some minimum level implied by the QMTC frontier) may be expressed as:

$$Q_d = t^{\epsilon} W^{\beta}, \qquad (1)$$

where W represents a vector of local demographic variables reflecting preferences, t is the tax-price of quality, ϵ is the tax-price elasticity, and β is a vector of elasticities corresponding to the elements of W. We choose the multiplicative form of the demand function to facilitate later estimation and interpretation of coefficients.

W includes the traditional types of demand parameters such as per capita income or wealth of the locality, education levels, age distribution, ethnic character, and other factors that might influence tastes or preferences for particular services, especially the quality of those services. t will be gauged in terms of local revenues that are raised per capita to support increments of quality. In practice, however, a technically precise estimate of tax-price per unit of quality is not available since quality units are not easily measurable. Thus, local service revenues per capita will be used as the appropriate proxy for the price local taxpayers would face in demanding quality increases.

Equation (1) is specified in units of quality. To derive the demanded additional expenditures (per capita) implicit in this quality relationship, we must multiply the demanded incremental quality level, Q_d, by a "perceived tax-price" which may be different from the local tax price, t. To see this, consider the following: If voters were completely blind to intergovernmental aid, they would behave as if local tax rates were the total prices for service quality, and hence demanded expenditures would be tQ_d, or simply the local share. On the other hand, if voters completely understood intergovernmental revenue flows, demanded expenditures would equal $(tG^{-1})\,Q_d$, where G is taken to be the ratio of local source revenues to total expenditures. In this case, constituents perceive the true price of service which is the local tax rate times $1/G$. Neither of these extremes is very likely. Instead, we argue that voters will recognize the existence of intergovernmental aid, though underestimate the full magnitude of the subsidy. Thus, total demanded incremental expenditures can be expressed as

$$D_d = (tG^{\eta})Q_d N \qquad (2)$$

where N represents the population of the community. Substituting for Q_d from Eq. (1), we obtain

$$D_d = (t^{1+\epsilon} G^{\eta})W^{\beta} N \qquad (3)$$

Note first that the tax-price elasticity of quality is equal to the coefficient value $1 + \epsilon$ minus one. This will be important to realize in interpreting estimated values in Chapters 4 and 5. We expect that ϵ itself will be negative (as tax-price increases, demanded quality decreases) while $1 + \epsilon$ may be positive.

We expect $-1 < \eta < 0$, reflecting underestimation of intergovernmental aid as the proportion of such aid increases relative to total expenditures. (Note that a value of $\eta < -1$ would indicate overestimation of grant funds by local voters while a value of $\eta > 0$ would mean that voters view state aid as taxing away service revenues. Both possibilities are unlikely, but the latter much more so than the former.) Thus, we argue that voters suffer from a type of "fiscal illusion" in that they tend to underestimate the real tax-price of public services. Roughly similar to Wagner (1976) who hypothesizes fiscal illusion to be the result of the complexity of intergovernmental revenue flows, we hypothesize a somewhat simpler relationship in which fiscal illusion increases as the proportion of local revenues decreases.

On the supply side, we adopt a simple model in which public officials begin their deliberations over the quality and costs of services they will offer with a perception of voter demands (Q_d, D_d). These demands are modified, however, in accord with differences in production costs across localities and with changes in accountability conditions affected by state aid. With regard to the latter, we postulate that higher levels of intergovernmental aid result in weaker voter monitoring, through the incentive as well as information effects discussed in Chapter 2 -- allowing local officials more leeway in setting quality and expenditure levels. Thus,

$$D_s = D_d \; S^{\gamma} G^{\pi} \qquad (4)$$

where S represents a vector of variables such as population density which are presumed to affect local costs of producing the service yet which are beyond the immediate control of the local officials, and π is an accountability parameter. We expect that $\pi < 0$, reflecting the hypothesis that expenditure deviations will increase as the level of intergovernmental aid increases (G declines). We base this contention on the various related considerations discussed in Chapter 2. First, as local revenues decrease in relative importance, revenue flows become less visible and less comprehensible to constituents, who in turn become less able to hold local officials accountable for expenditure of funds (the information effect). Second, again as the proportion of local revenues decreases, constituents find it less and less in their own interests to monitor carefully local agencies since an increasing proportion of any benefits from cost saving measures will be spread over the entire state (the incentive effect). Third, it seems reasonable to assume that distortionary effects will be correlated with the proportion of service revenues derived from external sources (that is, inversely related to G). That is, as grant funds increase, the distortionary effects of discriminatory subsidization of inputs, production strategies, or intermediate outputs, may also be expected to increase. Thus, the parameter π may contain a component due to distortionary effects as well as information and incentive effects. We may view distortion as another kind of incentive effect, albeit one which provides a "positive" inducement for local citizens to endorse (globally though not locally rooted) inefficiency as the proportion of funds from the outside increases. Nonetheless, all three effects should work in the same direction to make π more negative in value. To the contrary, the "supervision effect," that is, increases in oversight by the state, would theoretically reflect itself in the parameter as a separate accountability component that may be expected to increase (that is, improve efficiency) as the proportion of grant funds <u>increases</u> (that is, G declines). Thus, as described below, if the grant parameter turns out to be positive in sign, the supervision effect may be invoked as an interpretation of the accountability effect of the grant.

From equations (3) and (4) and dividing by N, we obtain

$$D = t^{1+\epsilon} W^{\beta} S^{\gamma} G^{\eta+\pi} \tag{5}$$

which states that the observed deviations from the QMTC frontier depend upon the tax-price constituents must pay for incremental quality, community tastes or preferences, local supply conditions, and the extent of intergovernmental aid.

Unfortunately, estimation of equation (5) cannot separate the differential effects of external aid (G) into fiscal illusion (η) and accountability (π) components. Nonetheless, equation (5) does provide a measure of the degree to which deviations from minimum expenditures for given output levels are related to demanded quality as opposed to grant induced inefficiency.

However, this issue bears looking at in more detail. Equation (5) is troublesome in the sense that the overall grant elasticity parameter $\eta + \pi$ is a compound one, representing the combined effects of fiscal illusion (η) in local citizens' estimations of external revenues, and accountability (π). Thus, we need to make some reasonable assumption about the value of η in order to discern the accountability/inefficiency effect of the grant. For example, consider the possibility that no accountability effect exists, that $\pi = 0$, and that the grant is perfectly perceived by local citizens ($\eta = -1$). In this case, the grant parameter will be $\pi + \eta = -1$. However, this would not indicate inefficiency despite the fact that equation (5) would show an inverse relationship between expenditure deviations and the proportion of local funding. Rather, it would indicate simply that the grant increases expenditure deviations which apparently go into quality improvements that are otherwise unaccounted for by the t and W factors of that equation, or possibly into extraordinary costs deriving from supply condition factors undetected through S.

Obviously, our modeling approach is designed to reject the latter interpretation; that is, we believe t, W, and S will capture nonefficiency determinants of expenditure deviation. Moreover, we have chosen services to study (see Chapters 4 and 5) where we believe quality variations will be less troublesome or can be investigated directly, and where sufficient data is available to account for such variations through the demand and supply condition factors in the model. Therefore, we are prone to assert that the proper interpretation of estimates of equation (5) should be based on the assumption that the fiscal illusion parameter is near zero, that is, that local citizens' perceptions of external funds are poor. For example, if $\eta = 0$, then an estimated result of $\pi + \eta = -1$ would mean that the hypothesized negative accountability effect of grants on efficiency does indeed hold, or, that $\pi = -1$.

In fact, it is important to consider how various outcomes of estimating the combined grant parameter $\eta + \pi$ should be interpreted in terms of our basic hypothesis that grants loosen the reins of local government accountability. Essentially, statistical estimation of equation (5) will yield a value for $\eta + \pi$ which we will call c. Thus,

$$\eta + \pi = c \tag{6}$$

It is useful to consider three mutually exclusive possible ranges for the estimated value of c:

The perverse case	$c > 0$	(7a)
The inelastic case	$0 > c > -1$	(7b)
The elastic case	$c < -1$	(7c)

We call the first possibility the "perverse case" because it means that overall, and contrary to our theoretical expectations, we have established a positive relationship between apparent inefficiency and the local share of service revenues. In the second (inelastic) case, the overall effect is the expected one -- apparent inefficiency is negatively related to local share, but with an elasticity of less than unity. In the third case, apparent inefficiency bears an elastic relationship to local share.

Equation (6) is plotted for the perverse case in Figure 3.2. Note the following interpretation for the various regions in this and the two subsequent graphs:

$\eta > 0$ (regions A and F): means that the "grant" is perceived (incorrectly) as negative by local citizens; that is, the state is seen to locally tax away rather than augment local service revenues;

$-1 < \eta < 0$ (regions B and E): means that the grant is underestimated by local citizens as a (positive) proportion of overall service revenues (as expected);

$\eta < -1$ (regions C and D): means that local citizens overestimate grant funds as a proportion of total service revenues;

$\pi > 0$ (regions A, B, and C): means that grant funds have a positive (constructive) effect on local accountability (contrary to expectations or consistent with the supervision effect);

$\pi < 0$ (regions D, E, and F): means that grant funds have a negative accountability effect (as expected).

FIGURE 3.2
The Perverse Case, $c > 0$

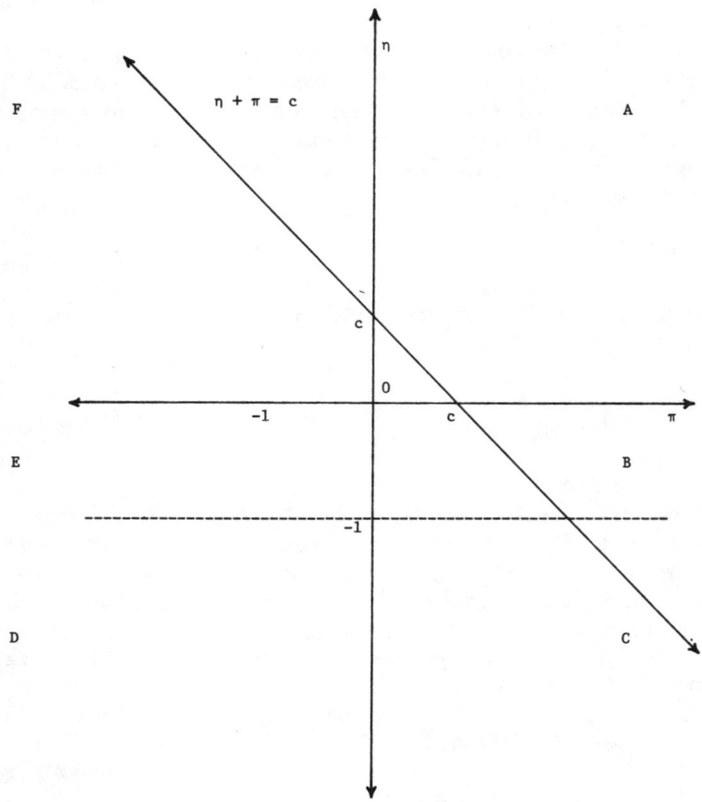

For the perverse case -- where c is empirically estimated to be a positive number -- the interpretation lies in regions A, B, C, or F. Hence, either:

The grant has a negative accountability effect, but contrary to expectations (and common sense) local voters perceive the grant as negative; <u>or</u>

Local citizens perceive the grant as positive (either under- or overestimating it) but that it has a negative accountability effect.

It follows, then, that an empirical estimate of c as a positive number would essentially constitute a refutation of our basic hypothesis, although the latter interpretation above would be consistent with the notion that the state supervision effects serve to overwhelm any loss of accountability incentives at the local level.

FIGURE 3.3
The Elastic Case, $c < -1$

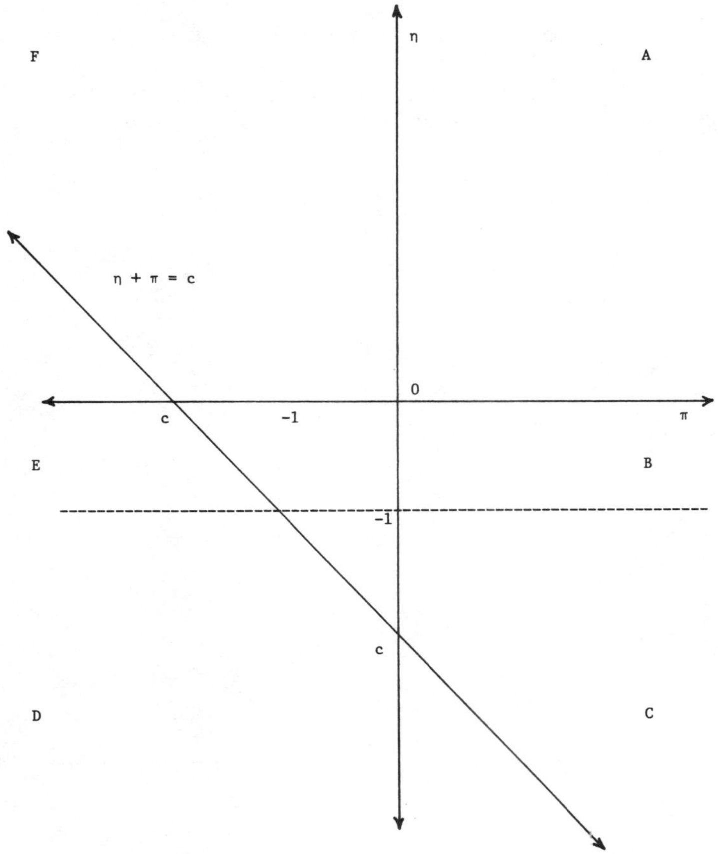

The elastic case is plotted in Figure 3.3. Here, there are four possibilities for interpreting a result that c is found to be less than -1:

1. the grant is overestimated by local citizens and exerts a positive effect on accountability (region C);
2. the grant is (less seriously) overestimated by local citizens and exerts a negative effect on accountability (region D);
3. the grant is underestimated by local citizens and exerts a negative influence on accountability (region E);
4. the grant is perceived as negative by local citizens but exerts a negative influence on accountability (region F).

Dismissing the last contingency (that is, a negative grant perception) as unrealistic, we can see that the second and third of these possibilities are essentially consistent with our basic hypothesis. The first possibility would constitute a refutation, except that one could argue that, if local citizens did greatly overestimate grant funds, then they might expect local officials to produce more than is feasible with the resources at hand, creating extraordinary pressures for local officials to become more efficient.

FIGURE 3.4
The Inelastic Case, $0 > c > -1$

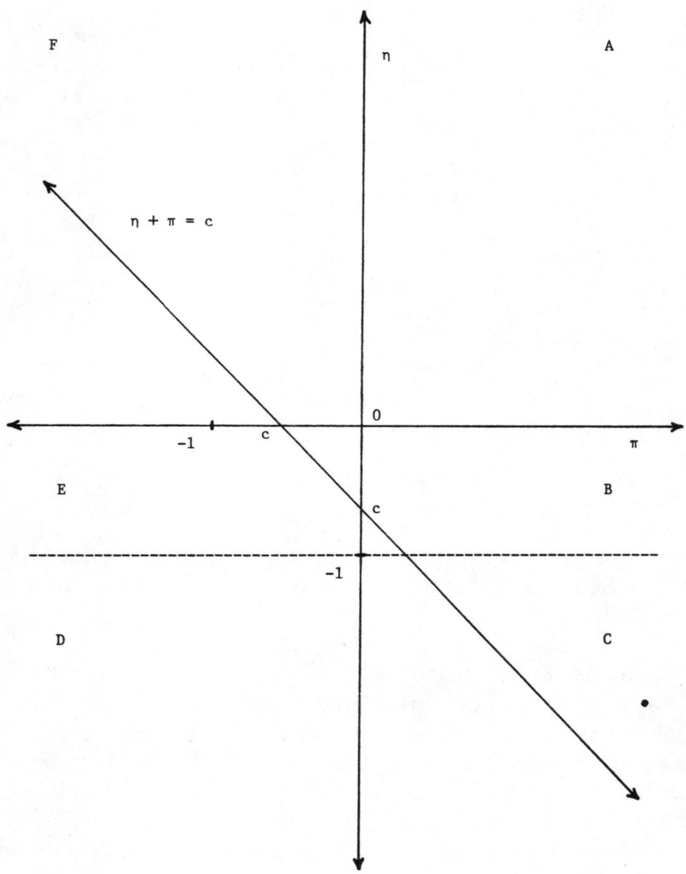

The inelastic case is plotted in Figure 3.4. Here, we again have four possibilities:

1. the grant is overestimated by local citizens and exerts a positive effect on accountability (region C);
2. the grant is underestimated by local citizens but has a positive effect on accountability (region B);
3. the grant is underestimated by local citizens and exerts a negative influence on accountability (region E);
4. the grant is perceived as negative in magnitude and exerts a negative influence on accountability (region F).

Here again we can dismiss the latter contingency as unrealistic. The first possibility could be interpreted as it was in the elastic case also: a highly overestimated grant would create local expectations that might pressure local officials into greater efficiency.

The most likely regions again, however, are where the grant is perceived as positive but is underestimated (contingencies 2 and 3). In the second instance, there is a positive accountability effect of the grant, contrary to expectations. The third possibility is completely consistent with the theory that grants loosen accountability. The closer the value of c approximates -1, the more likely is our hypothesis correct, as the segment of the line $\eta + \pi = c$ in region E increases and that portion of the line in region B decreases.

In summary, an empirical finding that $\eta + \pi = c > 0$ would be inconsistent with the theory suggested here, or more precisely, would indicate that the effects of state supervision overwhelm any losses in local accountability incentives due to grants. The other contingencies are more complex to interpret. It seems eminently reasonable to assume that citizens will neither view external grant funds as negative nor will they overestimate their magnitudes. Rather, they will most likely perceive some but not all of the incoming intergovernmental revenues for a given service, as in regions B and E where $0 < \eta < -1$. With this assumption, if c is found to be less than -1, then π must be less than zero and our hypothesized accountability effect holds. If, however, $0 < c < -1$ (the inelastic case) then the accountability effect can conceivably go either way.

Thus, it becomes necessary in this case to be more precise about our assumption regarding the value of η. If, as indicated above, we believe η is near zero -- that citizens perceive the existence of outside revenues poorly -- then our hypothesized accountability effect holds. Otherwise, it does not.

Looked at differently, we must argue effectively that, for whatever local service we study, we have eliminated quality variations (or extraordinary costs) or succeeded in capturing them in the demand and supply parameters (t, W, S) in equation (5). In such case, the deviations must represent inefficiency and hence the only thing that could account for a negative estimated relationship between G and D are losses due to the hypothesized accountability effects. In this case η must be near zero in order that $\pi < 0$.

SUMMARY

In summary, we have formulated a moderately effective test of the hypothesis that the proportion of external funds exerts a negative influence on local efficiency. If it obtains that $\eta + \pi = c > 0$, we can comfortably reject this hypothesis. If $c < -1$ we can comfortably accept it. If $0 < c < -1$ we can accept it also, contingent on the assumption that our data is based on observations that encompass minimal quality or extraordinary cost variation and/or these variations are captured by the demand and supply factors in the model.

4

PUBLIC LIBRARY SYSTEMS

DESCRIPTION OF THE SECTOR

There are approximately 8,500 public library systems in the United States, serving virtually all of the nation's population. These libraries are staffed by 36,000 professional librarians and have total operating expenditures of $1.32 billion of which $99 million or 12.9 percent is state aid and $67 million or 5.0 percent is federal aid (Improving State Aid to Public Libraries, 1977). Although some libraries do rely quite heavily on endowment income, the overwhelming proportion of public library funding is from local sources, chiefly local property taxes, and this is to remain so for the foreseeable future.

The history of development of public libraries in the United States reflects the changing reliance on different levels of government within our federal system for funding local public services. The first free public library in this country (there was no user charge for borrowing books) was founded in Peterborough, New Hampshire. This was followed quite closely in 1835 in New York State by the legislative authorization permitting local school districts to tax for the support of public libraries. New Hampshire in 1849 and Massachusetts in 1851 were the first states explicitly to authorize towns to appropriate monies for the establishment and support of public libraries. Similar authorizing legislation in other states laid the foundation for the growth of public libraries, although it was private philanthropy -- in particular the efforts of Andrew Carnegie -- which served as the catalyst. (See Shera, 1965, for a review of this early history.) The states became directly involved in funding public libraries in a very small way around the turn of the century as first Connecticut and later the other New

England and Middle Atlantic states gave nominal book purchasing grants to town public libraries. By the 1930s, many other states had followed this lead, often modifying the form of the grants to reflect per capita allocations to the library districts, to support equipment purchases or to support county or regional systems. The development of county and regional systems has been hastened in recent years, beginning in 1950, when New York State organized and partially supported a statewide network of cooperative public library systems.

The federal government's involvement in financing public library systems can be traced to the 1956 passage of the Library Services Act (LSA), intended ". . . to promote the further extension by the several states of public library services to the rural areas without such services or with inadequate services." (See Molz, 1976). However, only very limited funding was made available and those monies were targeted to localities with fewer than 10,000 people. Additional funding was made available in 1964 through the Library Services and Construction Act (LSCA) which extended the scope of the earlier act to all public library systems and to the construction of new or renovation of existing structures. A third component to this act was appended in 1966 to provide funds to encourage and support interlibrary cooperation. Today, however, 90 percent of all appropriations are for services provision, 10 percent for cooperative arrangements, and zero for construction or renovation. A recent development at the federal level has been the proposed National Library and Information Services Act (NLISA) which seeks to expand both the magnitude and scope of federal support to public libraries. The new federalism and the budget austerity of the Reagan administration make passage unlikely in the near future, leaving LSCA as the centerpiece of federal support through FY 1984 and probably FY 1985.

There are at least four factors which make public library systems at once extremely interesting yet quite difficult to analyze. The first is the absence of a uniform organizational structure in the way library services are produced across states. While the underlying concept of a library district, that is, a geographical area serviced by a library system, is common to all states, the natures of the districts themselves are quite different. In North Carolina, for example, there are 354 public libraries which provide access to public library services for all of the state's residents. Included among these 354 libraries are 15 regional (multi-county) libraries serving 49 counties and 51 county library systems, many with multiple branches, each serving one of the remaining 51 of the state's 100 counties. In addition to this county network, there exist 56 independent municipal library systems serving specific subcounty geographic regions. On the other hand, New York State relies to a much greater extent on more localized service. Here, library systems which are frequently coterminous with local school districts, tend to exhibit great variation in size, with populations served ranging from as few as 167 to as many as 3.3 million for the New York City Public Library System.

A second noteworthy aspect is the fact that different libraries are designed to do different things. In particular, some libraries are explicitly lending libraries while others couple that responsibility with the provision of reference materials, multimedia collections, and audio-visual equipment. Still others are document depositories and emphasize research almost to the exclusion of circulation. As with many public services, libraries are often characterized by multiple outputs or joint products, with outcome mix determined as much by the system's organizational structure (see below) as by cost and demand considerations. Hence, while the type of library is, as a rule, related to the size of the population and area it serves (the larger the population or area, the more research-oriented the library), organizational structure and hence output mix is typically determined by state policy.

In many states, individual libraries are parts of library systems with nested or hierarchical structures. At the lowest level are the smaller municipal libraries. On the second tier are the somewhat larger county libraries which also emphasize circulation but which provide ancillary services such as audio-visual equipment and reference materials. At the apex are regional libraries which oversee the operations of the county and municipal libraries. Generally, regional library functions are administrative though these libraries frequently serve as document depositories and research centers. Taken together, the hierarchy forms the library system, though it is important to note that decision making authority is much more centralized at the regional level in some states than in others. Since each library within the system is part of this larger whole, questions of costs, production, output mix, and efficiency should be viewed within the context of the system.

This is in sharp contrast to those states without such hierarchical systems wherein individual libraries, whether they be municipal, county, or regional, have more local autonomy. In these states, the library _is_ the system, and while libraries are frequently connected through interlibrary loan arrangements and other such informal networks, decision-making power remains vested with the local unit. As a result, systems tend to be less specialized in terms of output mix, to be smaller in terms of size of population served and total collections, and to have fewer branches, all other things being equal, than their hierarchical counterparts in other states.

In many states, however, the distinction between hierarchical and nonhierarchical organizational structures is not so clear. Indiana is a good example in which some elements of both structures exist. Here, public library services are provided through three separate components: (1) 239 local public library systems; (2) 9 area library service authorities (ALSA's) covering all 14 geographic planning regions of the state; and (3) the statewide Indiana Cooperative Library Services Authority (INCOLSA). The local library systems are fiscally autonomous and empowered with local taxing authority much like local school districts. They are governed by locally elected or appointed library boards and provide a range of services consistent with their sizes and local mandates. The ALSA's link local libraries within a specified region through interlibrary loan services, reference referrals, and continuing education programs. These services are provided only to member libraries which contract with the relevant ALSA's. INCOLSA, on the other hand, is a statewide agency which provides a wide range of technical services to local public libraries including information storage, retrieval, and dissemination. Both the ALSA's and INCOLSA are independent municipal corporations with only informal, though often significant, linkages to the statewide system of local libraries. As a result, while there is no legal basis for considering Indiana public libraries to be part of a larger hierarchical organizational structure, in practice the larger system, that is, the local public libraries together with the ALSA's and INCOLSA, exhibits many of the same characteristics of explicitly hierarchical structures in other states (Lane, 1982).

A further complicating factor is the prevalence of subcontracting among public library systems. The arrangement cited above between the ALSA's and the local public libraries in Indiana is quite common in other states. Typically, libraries will contract with other libraries higher up in the hierarchy for the provision of "higher order" services such as interlibrary loan arrangements or access to more extensive reference materials and other types of collections. This is especially common in rural and less urban areas of states where populations are small, and where it is economically infeasible for the local library to provide a full complement of services. A somewhat less common, though still significant, type of contractual arrangement exists in many states between library systems of similar rank. Under such arrangements, local libraries may contract with other local libraries serving different populations for many of the same services discussed above as well as others such as bookmobile services. In Idaho, for example, many of the smaller library systems are served in their entirety by bookmobile service contracted through other, larger local systems. One system, the Moscow-Latah district in Nez Perce County, was served through a Books-by-Mail program as recently as 1973-74. Such contractual arrangements make it that much more difficult to untangle the flow of funds within this sector from various levels of government.

The third factor is the wide variation in the magnitude and types of intergovernmental aid to libraries, especially state to local grants-in-aid. (See Grennon, 1981, for a listing and cataloguing of grants-in-aid.) Public library systems can receive as much as 100 percent of their operating revenues from state and federal sources, though, on average, they receive approximately 14 percent. At the extremes (excluding Hawaii), public libraries in North Dakota can only expect to receive 0.1 percent of their operating revenues from state sources while those in Georgia receive 45.8 percent on average. (Hawaii at 100 percent is unusual since it supports a single state run system.)

The great bulk of support for public libraries in the United States comes from local revenues and in particular local property tax receipts. However, states do provide dollars, and in many different ways. In Table 4.1, we categorize the library funding formulas of forty-one states according to their various components. As of FY 1978, eight states had no explicit state aid programs for local public libraries. They were Iowa, Louisiana, Mississippi, North and South Dakotas, Utah, Vermont, and Washington. Oregon had in place a discretionary program, and New Hampshire had a categorical library construction program on the books; however, neither state appropriated funds in 1978. Funding formulas in the remaining states can be characterized as being lump sum, matching, unit price reimbursement, or other (primarily competitive project grants), or some combination thereof. These, in turn, can be further categorized according to the specific parameters of the funding formulas. Lump sum grants are most often made in fixed amounts to the local library district, though many states have per capita, per square mile, and/or equalization components which differentially treat local library systems. For example, Maine and Nebraska provide $.10 per capita to local library systems, though Nebraska supplements this with a $400 foundation grant to each system. Georgia's aid system is slightly more complicated and far more lavish as each library system receives a foundation grant of $3,600 plus $1,000 for each county served, in addition to its $.40 per capita basic lump sum grant. Some states even incorporate equalization and tax effort provisions into their formulas. For instance, Pennsylvania has an equalization aid component of up to $.25 per capita for poorer districts while New Jersey's base level of support ranges from $.25 to $1.25 per capita depending upon local fiscal effort.

Matching ratios are either fixed or variable, that is, based upon the population or system characteristics of the local

TABLE 4.1
Characterization of Funding Formulas for 41 States
for Public Libraries

State	Formula Types: Lump Sum	Matching	Unit Price Reimbursement	Other
Alabama	x			
Arizona	x			x
Arkansas	x		x	x
California	x			x
Colorado				x
Connecticut	x		x	x
Delaware	x			
Florida	x	x		x
Georgia	x		x	x
Idaho	x			
Illinois	x			x
Indiana		x		
Iowa		(No funding formula)		
Kansas	x			
Kentucky	x			x
Louisiana		(No funding formula)		
Maine	x	x		x
Maryland		x		
Minnesota	x			x
Mississippi		(No funding formula)		
Missouri	x			x
Montana	x	x		x
Nevada				x
New Hampshire		(No funds allocated)		
New York	x	x		x
North Carolina	x	x	x	x
North Dakota		(No funding formula)		
Ohio	x		x	x
Oklahoma	x			
Oregon				x
Pennsylvania	x	x		x
Rhode Island	x			x
South Carolina	x			
South Dakota		(No funding formula)		
Texas	x			
Utah		(No funding formula)		
Vermont		(No funding formula)		
Virginia	x	x		
Washington		(No funding formula)		
West Virginia	x			
Wisconsin	x	x		

Source: Report by Bruno, 1980.

library district, such as wealth, and as a rule are closed-ended at ceiling levels which drastically reduce the average matching ratio below that contained in the legislation. For example, Virginia contributes $.35 for every local dollar expended, up to a maximum of $150,000. Since total local expenditures were approximately $23.2 million in Virginia in 1978, the effective average matching ratio was not .35, but rather .007 or 7 cents on every $10.00. Indiana is slightly more generous as its average matching ratio, with the existing ceiling of about $1,000,000, is .024. Wisconsin appears to have the most generous matching provision -- an open-ended 7 percent of operating expenditures.

Unit price reimbursements are generally made on the basis of approved operating expenditures in very specific categories such as personnel, travel, workshops, conferences, and bookmobiles, or in the support of very specialized services such as talking books centers (Georgia) or aid for services rendered to nonresidents (Connecticut). New Mexico, for example, provides $1,600 per bookmobile and a staff training grant of up to $200 per librarian -- all of this on top of differential basic grants for full and partial service systems and a variable per capita allocation.

The fourth factor, and one which cannot be overemphasized, is the remarkable degree of consistency across states in the manner in which library services are reported. Generally, a volume is a volume, a periodical a periodical, a microform a microform, a bookmobile a bookmobile, and a unit of circulation a unit of circulation regardless of the state, county, or locality in which the library is located. Perhaps this uniformity of definition and orderliness is endemic to public library systems or is simply a predominant characteristic of those who become librarians. Or perhaps it is the result of the American Library Association's efforts to standardize and professionalize the field of library sciences. Whatever its causes, the fact remains that the resulting interstate consistency makes the sector that much more attractive for empirical study vis à vis other public service sectors.

EMPIRICAL ANALYSES

With this background on public libraries, it is necessary to make a few simplifying assumptions for purposes of analysis. First, we assume that the predominant output made available by public library systems is "volume-hours," defined as the total number of volumes held by the system, multiplied by the number of hours each volume is made available to the public. Note that both volumes and hours are directly controlled by the library system itself. While others such as Getz (1980b), for example, define library output as circulation, our contention is that circulation is a measure of use rather than produced output and hence is a demand derivative of the basic service supplied by libraries, namely making volumes available to the general public. Clearly, if a library system is highly effective in meeting public demand, circulation will be high; thus, we view circulation more as an indication of the quality with which library services are provided than as a direct output of the system. Nonetheless, in subsequent analyses, we do experiment with three measures of output, volume-hours, circulation, and volume-hours adjusted for total circulation, just to see how sensitive our results are to the choice of measures.

In point of fact, libraries provide many more services than merely making books available to the public. Most libraries have extensive noncirculating collections which include reference materials, recordings, and audio-visual materials. In addition, the facility itself frequently serves a social function as a convenient conference or community center for town meetings or educational workshops. While we recognize these outputs of library systems, we also recognize that they account for the minority (less than 10 percent) of library expenditures. Further, it seems reasonable to assume that these other outputs would be roughly proportional to size -- volume-hours and traditional use (that is, circulation).

Second, we assume that the parameter which captures the productivity incentive effects of grant-in-aid formulas is the local share ratio or that portion of total expenditures derived from local sources. While there are obviously other important parameters of grant formulas, such as matching ratios, ceiling levels, and lump sum payments, the local share measure is a useful statistic since it is a composite average matching ratio for each library system. As such, it measures the local effort required on average and across all formula components to generate an additional dollar of expenditure. Our expectation is that it will capture the essence of formula differences across states and systems better than any other single index. It is also the one single grant index that can easily be compiled consistently across states and localities.

Finally, we assume that input factor markets relevant to public library operations are national in scope, and hence local library systems face similar input price schedules. This is clearly true for books, materials, and equipment which are produced and marketed nationally. However, salaries and benefits account for an average of 50 percent of library operating expenditures, and while there may be a national network for professional librarians, local economic factors are undoubtedly capitalized into wage rates and salary schedules.

Where such systematic differences in input price schedules do exist, for example, salary schedules or even bulk purchasing discounts for large systems, we assume that they can be controlled in our analyses with the inclusion of independent variables measuring differences in local production conditions (for example, population density).

The Data

The data for the empirical analyses which follow were collected from state fiscal reports for the year 1977-78 and from the 1977 U.S. Census City and County Data Book. In particular, state library data were examined for every state and accepted or rejected based upon two pragmatic considerations: (1) it must have been possible to compute volume-hours from the reported library data, and (2) the geographic area served by such systems had to be identifiable from the reports and had to be consistent with the geographic areas reported in the census. Effectively, the first criterion eliminated whole states and some systems within states for which volumes and/or hours were unavailable or untabulated by branch in multi-branch systems, while the second criterion eliminated those systems serving subcounty geographic regions or municipalities with populations less than 25,000.

It would be a mistake to view this sample of library systems as a random sample or for that matter as even representative of the 8,500 local public library systems in the country. Only 28 states are included in the data base, and, within these states, single branch systems are substantially over-represented. Since single branch systems are disproportionately smaller than multi-branch systems and located in more rural areas, the sample has a noticeable rural and suburban bias.

Generally, these published state reports provided a remarkably consistent set of data on inputs, outputs, expenditures, and revenues, though there were a fair number of inconsistencies and ambiguities that had to be resolved by phone conversations with state library officials. Included among these were clarifications of populations and areas served, disaggregations of expenditure categories, treatments of gift and nongovernmental revenue, and procedures used to compute full-time equivalent personnel. Also, these discussions were instrumental in untangling the flow of contractual payments among libraries in various states. As a result, we are quite confident that the data employed measure similar variables across states.

With respect to census data, we matched area served by library systems to units of census aggregation, that is, county or municipality, and extracted the relevant data. This matching process yielded a total of 773 "usable" public library systems in 28 states. However, in some analyses sample sizes reported are somewhat smaller since certain variables were occasionally unreported for some systems. The final column in Table 4.3 provides a frequency count of the full sample by state.

Quasi-Minimum Total Cost Frontier

The equation for the Quasi-Minimum Total Cost (QMTC) frontier was obtained by regressing total operating expenditures on volume-hours. The log-log specification was selected since it provided the best linearizing transformation of the data. We used operating expenditures and not total expenditures since capital costs are obviously lumpy over time and no state included in its annual report depreciation figures for existing capital stocks. This creates less of a problem than it may first appear since the only capital expenditures reported by library systems were construction costs. Book purchases, audio-visual equipment, and even vehicles other than bookmobiles were always treated as a part of operating expenditures. From the estimated regression equation, we then subtracted two standard deviations to obtain the QMTC frontier.

Figure 4.1 illustrates the relationship between the frontier and the estimated regression line. On the X and Y axes are the natural logs of volume-hours and total operating expenditures. The scatterplot demonstrates the highly linear relationship between the logs of the two variables. The estimated regression line is indicated by Line R and lies two standard deviations, or 1.18 units, above the QMTC frontier. Once the relationship has been linearized, the choice of how much to subtract from the regression line to obtain the frontier is necessarily arbitrary. We chose two standard deviations, which leaves approximately 2.5 percent of the observations below the frontier. In so doing, we feel we have avoided the unrealistically low outliers, and thereby have provided a "reasonable" lower bound standard of efficiency. The computed deviation of a library system is then equal to the vertical distance between it and the frontier.

The estimated regression coefficients and implied deviations are reported in Table 4.2 for three cases, the first using volume-hours as the output measure, the second using circulation, and the third using volume-hours but including circulation as a quality control adjustment factor. (Note that we use E, V, and C to represent total operating expenditures, volume-hours, and circulation, respectively.) It is interesting to note that there do not appear to be any economies of scale in the production of either volume-hours or circulation, a result which

FIGURE 4.1
Graphical Representation of QMTC Frontier and Regression Line

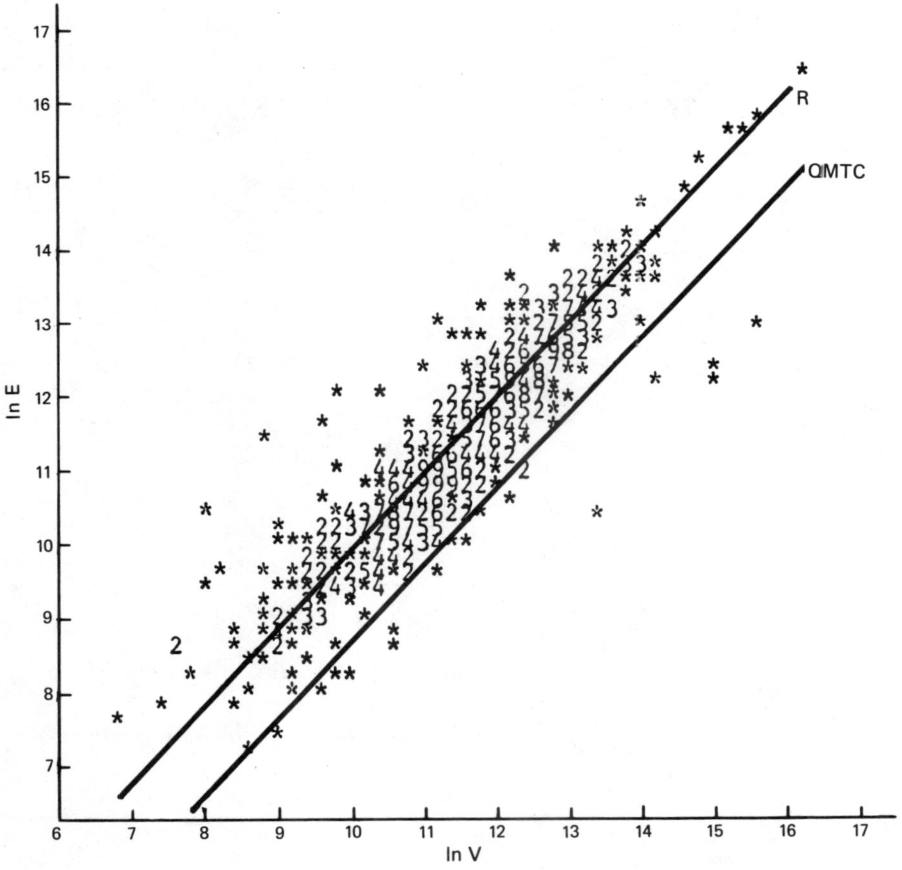

R -- Regression Line: $\ln E = .22 + .966 \ln V$

QMTC Frontier: $\ln E = -.96 + .966 \ln V$

Deviation from QMTC: $D = E - e^{(.22-2(.59))} V^{.966}$

appears to call into question efforts in many states to encourage library district consolidation. To put these frontier equations in better perspective, at the point of means it cost library systems on average \$.78 to produce a volume-hour and \$.33 to produce a unit of circulation. In comparison, systems on the frontier produce these same units for \$.24 and \$.13, respectively.

TABLE 4.2
QMTC Frontier Equations and Implied Deviations

Frontier Equations -- General Model: $E = e^{a}V^{b}C^{c}$ or $\ln E = a + b \ln V + c \ln C$						
Output Measure	$\hat{a}$	$\hat{b}$	$\hat{c}$	$\hat{\sigma}$	R^2	n
Volume-hours (V)	.22	.966 (60.0)	--	.59	.84	760
Circulation (C)	-.88	--	1.071 (71.4)	.51	.87	760
Vol. hrs. with circulation	-1.02	.400 (13.7)	.680 (21.5)	.45	.89	760

Implied Deviations -- General Model: $D = E - e^{(\hat{a} - 2\hat{\sigma})} V^{\hat{b}} C^{\hat{c}}$ (in dollars)	
Volume-hours (V)	$D = E - e^{(.22-2(.59))} V^{.966}$
Circulation (C)	$D = E - e^{(-.88-2(.51))} C^{1.071}$
Vol. hrs. with circulation	$D = E - e^{(-1.02-2(.45))} V^{.40} C^{.68}$

t-statistics are in parentheses

What is particularly interesting regarding the calculated deviations from the QMTC frontier is that no one state determines the frontier. Referring to Table 4.3, note that of the 28 states, fully 12 have library systems on (or below) the frontier, a remarkable scattering considering that by construction only 2.5 percent of the observations should fall within this region. This result is qualitatively similar for the other two output measures. There are, however, significant differences in the mean proportion deviations (defined as deviation divided by total operating expenditures) by state as illustrated in Table 4.4. For all output measures, the state means show significant differences though rank orderings of these state means are generally preserved. High average expenditure states are high regardless of choice of output measure, a fact which makes the choice of an output measure less agonizing.

TABLE 4.3
Frequency Counts of Percent Deviation from QMTC Frontier--
Output Measure is Volume-Hours

State	<0%	0-25%	26-50%	51-75%	>75%	# of Systems
AL	0	1	2	16	20	39
CA	0	0	0	2	14	16
CO	1	3	2	16	7	29
DE	0	0	0	2	0	2
FL	2	0	1	7	10	20
ID	1	0	1	14	19	35
IL	2	1	4	38	31	76
IN	0	1	6	10	7	24
IA	3	1	8	41	13	66
KY	1	2	24	26	9	62
LA	0	0	0	7	6	13
MI	0	1	3	16	13	33
MN	1	0	2	24	15	42
MS	0	1	0	6	1	8
MO	0	3	4	11	0	18
MT	1	3	6	17	10	37
NV	0	0	0	3	6	9
NH	0	0	0	3	0	3
NM	1	0	4	13	5	23
NY	4	0	1	20	19	44
ND	0	0	3	10	1	14
OH	0	0	5	23	5	33
PA	0	1	5	44	20	70
SD	0	1	0	1	2	4
VT	0	0	0	1	0	1
VA	2	0	3	11	3	19
WA	3	0	0	1	11	15
WV	0	1	6	7	4	18

TABLE 4.4
Comparison of State-wide Mean Deviations per Dollar of Total Expenditures

State	Output Measure		
	Vol. Hrs.	Circulation	Vol. Hrs. with Circulation
MT	.47	.30	.32
VA	.51	.42	.51
KY	.52	.38	.40
IA	.55	.40	.49
WV	.55	.46	.43
NY	.57	.32	.60
NV	.58	.50	.53
ND	.59	.48	.50
CO	.59	.49	.50
SD	.61	.45	.61
IN	.62	.48	.55
MO	.63	.53	.66
OH	.65	.50	.51
FL	.65	.50	.57
IL	.66	.52	.60
PA	.67	.51	.57
NM	.67	.47	.59
MI	.68	.55	.65
DE	.69	.55	.51
MN	.70	.60	.58
ID	.71	.65	.61
AL	.74	.64	.59
LA	.74	.67	.65
VT	.75	.66	.71
NH	.77	.73	.71
WA	.81	.69	.65
CA	.83	.74	.72
Grand mean	.63	.50	.55
F	1.770	1.108	4.125
Significance	.009	.322	.000

Sink Analysis

We define three "sinks" consistent with reported expenditure categories across states. They are:

1. H1 -- includes all expenditures on wages, salaries, and fringe benefits.
2. H2 -- includes all expenditures for library materials, for example, books, periodicals, microforms, and audio-visual materials.
3. H3 -- includes all other operating expenditures such as equipment purchases, utilities, maintenance, and all other nonmaterial purchases.

On average, 55 percent of public library system operating expenditures fall into H1, 20 percent into H2, and 25 percent into H3. These averages hide the substantial and significant interstate differences in expenditure patterns. For example, systems in Virginia and Indiana report only 36 percent and 44 percent of operating expenditures in H1, while at the other extreme those in New Hampshire and California report 71 percent and 65 percent, respectively. There is, however, only scant evidence to suggest that any one of the sinks absorbs more of the deviations than either of the other two. While library systems do exhibit wide variations in how they spend their money, there is little reason to believe that on average the choice of input mix determines deviations from the QMTC frontier.

At the margin, however, there do appear to be differences in the relative productivities of each of the three sinks. We regressed the magnitude of the deviations for the three output measures on H1, H2, and H3. The results are shown in Table 4.5. All estimated coefficients in each specification were significant at better than the .01 level.

These coefficient estimates should be compared to the average expected effect of an additional dollar spent, since by construction the average library system is almost three times more costly than a system on the frontier. This means that any increase in total expenditures will result in an absolute increase in the size of that system's deviation, the magnitude of which depends upon the relative slopes of the frontier and the regression line, reported in Table 4.2, from which it was derived. In the last row of Table 4.5, we report these average expected effects calculated at the point of means for each specification. Clearly, expenditures for materials and other inputs yield a much higher return at the margin than expenditures for salaries and benefits. This finding can be compared to Getz's (1980a) findings in his study of the New York City Public

Library system. Getz found that the system could be made more cost effective by reducing the number of branches while expanding the number of hours open and the sizes of the collections in the remaining branches. While the latter result is consistent with our findings, the former may or may not be depending upon the input mix used by libraries to "produce" hours open. Unfortunately, available data does not permit us to take the next step to determine whether these low yields on H1 result from higher than average salary schedules, higher than average labor-output ratios, or both. Nevertheless, it does appear that, at the margin, high expenditure library systems could reduce their unit costs and hence move closer to the frontier by altering their expenditure pattern (input mix) in favor of materials and equipment and away from personnel.

TABLE 4.5
Coefficient Estimates for Marginal Productivity of Additional Expenditures by Budget Category by Output Measure

Budget Category	Output Measure: Volume Hours	Output Measure: Circulation	Output Measure: Vol. Hrs. with Circulation
H1--Salaries and benefits	.912 (46.79)	1.085 (58.86)	.977 (65.54)
H2--Materials	.601 (4.85)	-.553 (4.49)	-.356 (3.66)
H3--Equipment and other miscellaneous	.678 (16.25)	.492 (12.29)	.449 (14.07)
Constant	-12842	133	-114
R^2	.991	.991	.994
Average expected effect at the means	.690	.640	.600

(n = 601 in all cases)
t-statistics in parentheses

Determinant Analysis

Our discussion in Chapters 2 and 3 identified several possible determinants of a library system's deviation from the quasi-minimum total cost frontier. To reiterate, library systems may spend different amounts of money to provide similar levels of services as a result of variations in local production conditions, the presence of multiple outputs or joint products and/or local constituent demand for better quality services, or lastly waste or operating inefficiencies.

There are both reasons why we would expect, and would not expect, to see variations in local production conditions for public library services. We might not expect to see much in the way of local variations (independent of size effects) since service provision is pretty much standardized through the efforts of the American Library Association and since most library materials are produced for national and not local markets. On the other hand, service modes may vary according to the geography of the area served. Low density areas may find it more economical to utilize bookmobiles rather than additional branches as is typically the case in higher density, metropolitan areas. Also, certain input prices, primarily wage rates and salary schedules, may exhibit significant local variations, thereby contributing to a system's observed deviation from the QMTC frontier. In our empirical analyses, we attempt to control for both effects through the inclusion of the number of branches in the system as a loose measure of organizational structure and population density to control for differences in input prices.

A persistent concern which we have is that, by focusing on any one output such as volume-hours or circulation, we may fail to consider other dimensions of library services which may account for some of the observed deviation. Unfortunately, data on most of these other dimensions, for example, in-library use, reference questions asked, or public forums held, is spotty and difficult to interpret. We were, however, able to develop two reasonably consistent indicators of other services provided -- reference materials and the audio-visual holdings of the library system -- which we included as independent regressors in the deviation equation. In every instance the variables proved insignificant, in large part, we believe, because of their correlations with system size and their proportional relationships with circulation. (We do not report the results of the models with these variables included since their continued inclusion is certain to bias all coefficient estimates in the model.)

The issue of quality is even more perplexing than that of joint products since it is that much more difficult to observe and hence to control. There are no direct measures of quality available in standard state data sources, and hence levels of quality must be inferred through the characteristics of the local constituency. The argument we make is that local voters have a demand for quality of services which is manifested through the political process and which is determined, in a traditional economic framework, by prices and ability to pay. In accordance with our discussion in Chapter 2, we consider the local tax-price of the library system, proxied as locally raised revenues per capita, as the price voters face for improved quality of services. We measure income effects by median family income and by median values of single family, owner-occupied housing of the population served by the library system. We accord these two variables their usual interpretations, though we do acknowledge some ambiguities since they may be related to use (circulation) as well as to expenditures for better quality. If per capita circulation is higher in wealthier communities, as one might expect, and if unit costs are pretty much average, then the system will, by definition, be more cost-effective.

Finally, we include a grant parameter, defined as the local share of total revenues, as a determinant of waste or operating inefficiencies.

We regressed the observed deviations, expressed in dollars per capita, on the foregoing set of independent variables. The results are reported in Table 4.6. Since the log-log specification was used, the coefficient estimates are elasticities. The equations are all very significant, and the coefficient estimates generally conform to expectations. The price elasticity of demand for library quality is close to -0.7 and when significant the other demand variables carry the expected signs. Since libraries draw most heavily upon local property tax revenues, median property values are arguably a better measure of "income" or ability to pay than are median family incomes, though the two variables are strongly correlated. The estimated coefficients of approximately 0.2 in all three specifications suggest that per capita spending for public libraries varies much less across districts of varying wealths than it does for other public services such as education. Somewhat surprisingly, the deviations from the frontier are not related to population density and hence arguably not to cost differentials across systems. Also, it seems that library systems with fewer branches are less cost effective in providing volume-hours, though the coefficients are insignificant in all three cases.

The coefficient on the local share proportion is highly significant and has the expected sign -- the higher the local share, the lower the per capita deviation from the QMTC frontier -- indicating (with the appropriate assumptions of high fiscal illusion and lack of uncaptured quality or cost variations in the data, see Chapter 3) the presence of information, incentive, and possibly distortion effects. Furthermore, the magnitude of this coefficient is substantial, suggesting an elasticity of about 0.34. This means that a 1 percent increase in local share (from 0.68 to 0.74 at the average value) or the equivalent of $17,900 for this average system and a comparable reduction in intergovernmental aid will reduce the per capita deviation from the frontier by 3.4 percent or roughly $.28 per capita for the average library system. Multiplying this by 45,735, the average population served by the sampled systems yields a mean savings of $12,805.80 or 5.01 percent of the average system's total operating budget. As this 10 percent increase in local share will impose a $17,900 additional local burden for this average library system (the loss in intergovernmental aid), it is important to note that fully 72 percent ($12,805.80) of the $17,900 can be met by reductions in operating inefficiencies through movement closer to the QMTC frontier. That is, if the locality is able to fully exploit the potential efficiency gains, a loss of $17,900 in intergovernmental aid can be offset by an increase of only $5094.20 of locally raised revenue, without changing the level of services provided.

TABLE 4.6
Regression Estimates of the Determinants of the Deviations (in dollars per capita) from the QMTC Frontier

Independent Variables	Output Measures: Volume Hours	Output Measures: Circulation	Output Measures: Vol. Hrs. with Circulation
Demand related:			
Tax-Price (1+ε)	.306	.288	.281
	(32.30)	(28.16)	(26.31)
Median income	-.002	.064	-.028
	(.01)	(1.46)	(.62)
Median property value	.197	.156	.229
	(6.39)	(4.68)	(6.57)
Supply conditions:			
Population density	.006	.001	-.003
	(1.28)	(.56)	(.64)
Number of branches	-.008	-.022	-.010
	(.31)	(.04)	(1.14)
Grant-related:			
Local share	-.349	-.342	-.327
	(23.86)	(20.95)	(19.21)
Constant	-.225	-.433	-.275
F	353.21	269.93	237.44
R^2	.74	.68	.66
n	749	749	749

t-statistics in parentheses

Alternatively, consider this more complicated situation in which the state supplements its aid to library systems by a $10,000 lump sum grant, and these systems respond by reducing local effort. This increase in state aid of $10,000 may elicit a reduction in local revenues of $10,000 if there is complete substitution, a reduction of less than $10,000 if there is partial substitution, or no reduction at all if there is no substitution. We define these cases as $\tau = 0$, $0 < \tau < 1$, and $\tau = 1$, respectively. What is very disturbing is that the local response, if $\tau < 1$, serves to aggravate the reduction in the local share caused by the supplemental grant, and, in so doing, further increases a system's deviation from the frontier. In fact, for reasonable estimates of τ, the increase in deviation may actually be larger than the increase in total expenditures!

TABLE 4.7
Effect of a $10,000 Lump Sum Increase in State Aid on Total Expenditure, Local Share, and Deviation from the QMTC Frontier

τ	Increase in Total Expenditure	Change in Local Share	Increase in Total Deviation	Increase in Deviation as Percent of Increase in Total Expenditure
0	0	-.039	$7,313	–
.20	$2,000	-.036	$6,810	341%
.40	4,000	-.034	$6,296	154%
.60	6,000	-.031	$5,789	96%
.80	8,000	-.028	$5,290	66%
1.00	10,000	-.025	$4,798	48%

τ is the increase in total expenditure resulting from a dollar increase in state aid.

To illustrate this, let $\tau = .40$, which is within the range estimated by Gramlich and Galper (1973). A $10,000 grant will then increase total expenditures by only $4,000 since the locality will reduce local revenues by $6,000. The net effect will be a reduction in the proportion local share of .034 from .680 to .646 for the average system. Such a reduction will increase the per capita deviation by $.137 and total deviation by $6,296, or by 54 percent more than the increase in total expenditures. This is shown in Table 4.7 for various values of τ between zero and one. It is only for large values of τ (in excess of .60) that the increase in expenditures resulting from an increase in state aid will outweigh increases in deviations or operating inefficiencies. For small values of τ, for example, Gramlich and Galper's estimate of 0.4, where state aid essentially substitutes for local effort, total expenditures will generally increase; however, less output will be produced. The increase in deviation from the QMTC frontier stemming from the drop in local share will, dollar for dollar, more than offset the increase in total expenditures. The consequences of a well intentioned "optimizing" grant program intended to stimulate local service production may in fact be an increase in total expenditures, purchased, however, at the cost of an absolute reduction in total output or services provided! This is a likelihood which the fiscal federalism literature has heretofore ignored.

SUMMARY

Within the context of our estimated model, the inefficiency effects of intergovernmental aid are quite profound. In fact, under reasonable assumptions regarding the behavioral response of local government units to changes in intergovernmental aid levels, changes in such aid can result in dollar for dollar changes in operating efficiency. If aid levels are increased, for example, more money will be spent, but more output will not necessarily be produced. Of course, these results are valid only to the extent that our procedures have adequately controlled for existing quality differences across localities and are applicable only to local public libraries. We have discussed this former issue at length in this chapter and are ourselves convinced that all meaningful quality variations which might have existed have been controlled for. With regard to the latter issue, we now turn our attention to public school transportation to see if similar results emerge in a second instance wherein a service is locally provided using various combinations of locally raised revenues and intergovernmental aid.

5

SCHOOL BUS TRANSPORTATION SYSTEMS

PUPIL TRANSPORTATION SYSTEMS

State support for pupil transportation has historically lagged state support for public education. Massachusetts, in 1869, was the first state to authorize the expenditure of public funds for pupil transportation; however, the authorization covered only local funds and did not include state aid. Indeed, prior to 1910, only New Jersey and Wisconsin (with lump sum grants) and Connecticut and Vermont (with matching grants) had state aid programs in this area.

School district consolidation, the secondary school movement, and the coming of the automobile era provided the impetus for increased state involvement in the financing of pupil transportation. By 1933, 32 states provided some form of state pupil transportation aid, and by 1948, 40 states were aiding local school districts' transportation systems through components to the basic state education aid programs, through special lump sum grants to localities, through equalization formulas, or through some combination of these methods. By 1978-79, New Hampshire was the only state not providing state aid for pupil transportation. This growth in state support is reflected in the increases in the numbers of students transported and total costs (see Table 5.1). As the numbers in this table indicate, school bus transportation has become an integral and expensive component of our public education system.

Accompanying the growth in this sector has been a voluminous body of literature surrounding the financing of school bus transportation programs. The key issue in the early part of this literature was whether state aid should be related to incurred or expected costs, where the latter was generally estimated as a

TABLE 5.1
Selected Public School Transportation Data for the United States, 1954-55 to 1977-78

Year	Number of Pupils Transported (1,000s)	Number of Buses Employed (1,000s)	Total Operating Expenditures ($1,000s)
1954	9,510	154	329,035
1955	10,199	160	356,349
1956	10,683	165	362,751
1957	11,343	171	419,539
1958*	12,021	176	441,402
1959**	12,700	180	474,202
1960	13,106	186	505,754
1961	13,687	191	540,168
1962	14,247	195	578,017
1963	15,559	200	612,310
1964	N/A	N/A	N/A
1965	16,423	211	696,325
1966	16,685	222	763,600
1967	17,272	231	822,595
1968	18,468	238	901,353
1969	18,753	240	966,135
1970	19,191	246	1,178,910
1971	20,047	258	1,324,740
1972	20,792	263	1,407,472
1973	21,170	272	1,537,148
1974	22,938	283	2,000,991
1975	22,803	312	2,285,840
1976	23,156	298	2,666,446
1977	21,924	315	2,880,513

* Alaska added in 1958 and subsequent years.
** Hawaii added in 1959 and subsequent years.
Source: National Association of State Public Transportation Directors.

function of the geography and/or population density of a school district. Three generic funding formulas emerged: (1) reimbursement of cost per pupil based upon population density or other factors outside the district's immediate control; (2) reimbursement based upon cost per bus route at a rate which may vary by route length or bus size; and (3) reimbursement based upon allowable budget items. The debate represents one of the first instances in which the relationship between grants-in-aid and efficiency is acknowledged. On the one hand, those favoring straight cost reimbursement argued that the cost functions for pupil transportation systems varied so substantially across districts that to not simply reimburse costs would be to award state aid in a capricious fashion, rewarding and penalizing districts for factors over which they have no control. Checks on the system would be provided through frequent and stringent state audits of local expenditures. The opposing camp argued that to simply reimburse costs would encourage local inefficiency since the local price for school bus transportation would be effectively zero. Instead, they argued that school districts should pay a proportion of total costs (via matching grants), and that they should be encouraged to operate at minimum costs through expenditure targets and/or limitations.

Judging from the recent literature and in particular the National Education Finance Project (NEFP) studies in the early 1970s, the efficiency arguments appear to have won at least the philosophical debate. Recent formula changes or recommendations for such changes in Kentucky, South Dakota, Missouri, Utah, and Minnesota, for example, have incorporated explicit density adjustment factors; however, most states continue to rely upon unit price reimbursement, matching ratios, or some other miscellaneous criteria.

With respect to the first category, reimbursement varies by unit, for example, per student transported, by miles driven, by vehicles used or purchased, or by some combination of these; and by rate, that is, fixed or variable, (as a function of either population density or equalized assessed valuation). For example, Alabama reimburses approximately 80 percent of local transportation expenditures based upon a population density adjustment factor computed as a best fit curve relating unit costs to density of school districts. More efficient districts, that is, those districts which do better than expected given their densities, receive higher levels of state aid than do those districts which do worse than expected. Ohio's formula is even more complicated in that it differentiates among service providers. District owned and operated buses receive the greater of $43.00 per pupil or $.39 per approved mile, while contractor owned and operated buses receive slightly more, the greater of $49.00 per pupil or $.43 per approved mile. Public utility carriers (typically metropolitan transit systems in major cities) get reimbursed at the rate of $60.00 per pupil. In addition, for the very remote and low density districts, parents or guardians can collect up to $85.34 per pupil per year for arranging private transportation. These figures are set so as to fund roughly 50 percent of local school district pupil transportation operating costs. Ohio also has a bus purchasing aid program through which local school districts can get reimbursed at rates ranging from 28 percent to 80 percent (based upon district assessed valuation) for school bus purchases.

The matching ratio aid formulas tend to be less complicated, though they also generally have multiple components. For instance, Idaho reimburses allowable expenditures (including driver and mechanic wages and benefits, insurance costs, fuel, lubricants, minor and routine repair and replacement parts and contracted costs) at 85 percent of expenditures. Expenditures can be included for only those pupils living outside of a 1.5 mile radius from their schools, and only public school children are eligible. In addition, if payment is made to a parent or guardian in lieu of school district transportation, payment is limited to a maximum of $10.00 per month plus $.15 per mile. Massachusetts has similar provisions as Idaho regarding allowable students and expenditure categories, however, it is nominally more generous as its matching ratio is 90 percent. Its effective rate is much lower, however, since the program is closed-ended and appropriations have not kept pace with expenditures. (The present average matching ratio is between 45 and 50 percent.) North Carolina is among the most generous of states as its matching rate is fully 100 percent of approved operating expenditures. Students must live a minimum of 1.5 miles from school, and all reimbursements are made based upon statewide average rates for such categories as salaries, parts, and repairs.

Finally, there are those states whose formulas do not easily fit into either of the above two categories. Georgia, for example, has locally owned and operated buses under the direction of strong state supervision. Reimbursements are made based upon rates which vary according to district location, that is, Mountain, Metropolitan, Mid-Georgia, or South Georgia, with metropolitan districts receiving about 30 percent higher reimbursement rates than the lowest districts in South Georgia. Rhode Island does not have a separate formula to calculate reimbursement for transportation; rather, transportation costs are reimbursed as part of the general aid to education formula. Interestingly, this aid formula is such that under certain conditions (which two districts met in 1976-77) the reimbursement rate can actually exceed 100 percent.

In some important respects, school bus transportation is very much like public library services. There is no uniform organizational structure which provides school bus transportation, as the organization of the school districts themselves varies from state to state and even within states. While most states rely upon the local school district (whose boundaries tend to conform with municipal borders), some southern states have county school districts that are of much larger geographic areas and encompass multiple local governments. Even within a state, there are differences arising from consolidation arrangements and district mergers. Generally, such consolidations involve the merging of one entire district with another, though there are instances in which consolidation preserves local district boundaries for the lower grades but merges districts for secondary education purposes.

Second, school districts, as with library systems, are designed to do different things. For example, in many states special districts exist to educate those with severe learning disabilities. These districts are similar to consolidated districts as they serve many local school districts within a geographic area. As a result, their transportation needs are likely to be quite different from typical districts, and their existence is likely to influence the transportation systems of those local districts they serve. School districts also have a certain degree of flexibility in terms of how they provide school bus transportation services. Staggered school hours, distances between bus stops, time spent on the bus, the use of contracted or municipal carriers, and even the location of school buildings are all parameters of the school bus transportation system over which local school districts exert some degree of control. Further, these are all factors affecting the quality of service provision that are likely to be unobserved since they are not reported in traditional input and output statistics.

A notable difference between the two services, however, is the extent to which each is characterized by multiple outputs or joint products. We noted earlier that library services exhibit a high degree of jointness in their provision, for example, circulation, reference materials, A-V materials, and so on. School bus transportation, on the other hand, is much more uniform across local providers and is much less characterized by jointness of outputs. The primary output of the transportation system, that is, transporting a student to and from school, accounts for the overwhelming majority of local expenditures and service provision. While some districts may also use their bus fleets for such activities as field trips, outings, and athletic events, such use accounts for a small fraction of services provided by the school districts. Conceivably, even this small fraction of services could cause trouble, however, since school districts generally report only expenditures incurred in providing these ancillary services. There is no systematic reporting of the magnitude of the services provided.

EMPIRICAL ANALYSES

Our empirical analysis of school bus transportation parallels that presented above for public library systems. We assume that the local share or that proportion of total expenditures derived from local sources reflects the nature of formula differences across states and local districts, and that the important input factor markets such as buses, bus drivers, fuel, and parts are such that local districts face similar input prices. The differences that are present in price schedules reflect cost-of-living differences only, which we assume are strongly correlated with population density and hence controlled for by including density in the estimated models.

The output of school bus transportation is the transporting of a regular student to and from school over the course of an academic year. We assume this output to be relatively homogeneous, first because it is the predominant output of such systems and second, because the opportunity for quality differences across localities is likely to be small. While school districts often have control over certain parameters such as the location and frequency of bus stops, they are generally substantially constrained by state and federal rules and regulations governing the specifications and uses of equipment and qualifications of personnel. The busing of a student in one school district is pretty much the same as the busing of a student in any other school district.

The Data

School bus transportation data was collected from six states -- Kentucky, Maryland, Massachusetts, Michigan, New Mexico, and Texas from published state annual reports and from computerized data files maintained by the respective state education departments for the 1977-78 academic year. These states were chosen on the basis of the availability of data and consistency of variables and definitions across states. While we would have liked to have been able to include additional states in our analysis, detailed examination of the available data in other states revealed a variety of incompatibility problems. Among these were differing definitions of expenditure categories and treatments of capital outlays, an inability to disentangle consolidations, jointures, and mergers of school districts, correlations of aid formulas and thus local shares with school district wealth, and an inability to identify and factor out the transportation of private school students and/or special education and handicapped students.

Many of the data problems we encountered which caused us to exclude a state from our sample were of the ordinary variety. For example, Ohio data was not available since the state was in the process of computerizing its record keeping. Other data problems were extraordinary. For example, in Arizona, state records did not contain complete enrollment data in many of the consolidated districts since the state was not particularly concerned with the flow of pupils but rather with only their number; in New York, we found many districts busing more students than they reported enrolled since the state data indiscriminantly aggregated public and private school students; and in New Jersey, both of the above problems existed. In addition, other states were excluded because their state aid formulas contained explicit and significant wealth equalization components which reimbursed poorer districts at higher levels than richer districts. As a result, price and income effects associated with grants-in-aid would be correlated with demand variables thereby confounding our subsequent empirical analyses of the efficiency effects of intergovernmental aid.

The six states which were included provided us with 1,575 school districts -- 145 in Kentucky, 24 in Maryland, 176 in Massachusetts, 414 in Michigan, 85 in New Mexico, and 731 in Texas. These represent close to census samples in the respective states. Certain districts were eliminated based upon missing or obviously faulty or misreported data while others were eliminated if their transportation systems were too heavily weighted (greater than 50 percent) towards special or handicapped students. Fifty percent was an arbitrary cut-off point which had the effect of excluding school districts established for the explicit purpose of educating those students with special education needs. Clearly, such districts are educationally different from regular school districts and so are their transportation needs.

Additional data was extracted from the 1970 Census of Population and Housing (Fifth Count tallies by school district). Generally, the process of matching census and state education department data went quite smoothly. However, there were a number of instances in which school districts existing in 1970 had been consolidated or otherwise phased out by 1977-78 and vice versa. In such instances, these districts were removed from the sample. The census data provided us with demographic information for each of the school districts, which, though somewhat outdated, was nevertheless the best available.

Quasi-Minimum Total Cost Frontier

In deriving the Quasi Minimum Total Cost (QMTC) frontier, we regressed total operating plus depreciation expenditures on the number of students transported. Operating expenditures were very straightforward and included wages and fringe benefits, fuel, maintenance, and parts. In all instances, these figures were reported in the state statistical reports. The depreciation figures, on the other hand, were not so reported, and hence we had to compute depreciation for each school district based upon the numbers and types of buses in district fleets, the statewide average purchase prices of each bus type, and their respective depreciation schedules. The cost and depreciation schedules were obtained from the state departments of education and, while there were some differences across states, these differences were not judged to be important. As was the case with public libraries, the log-log specification was chosen since it represented the best linearizing transformation of the data. In addition, we included the log of the "transported density" of each school district, defined as the number of students transported divided by the area of the district, on the right-hand side to control for differences in geography which clearly would influence total costs. The results of the regression and the implied deviations are shown in Table 5.2.

TABLE 5.2
QMTC Frontier Equations and Implied Deviations

Frontier Equations --
General Model: $E = e^{a}TR^{b}DN^{c}$

	Coefficient	T-Value
No. of pupils transported (TR)	.98	93.9
Transported density (DN)	-.10	13.6
Constant	5.30	
R^2	.91	
$\hat{\sigma}$	.37	
n	1561	

Implied Deviations --
General Model: $D = E - e^{(\hat{a} - 2\hat{\sigma})} TR^{\hat{b}}DN^{\hat{c}}$ (in dollars)

$D = E - e^{(5.3-2(.37))}TR^{.98}DN^{-.10}$

It is interesting to note that the coefficient on the number of students transported is very close to 1.0, suggesting that there are very few economies of scale available in school transportation once density has been controlled for. This is not a surprising finding since school districts are able to expand or contract virtually all aspects of their transportation operations through the use of various size buses, shared overhead with district administration, part-time employment of bus drivers, and contracted maintenance. Surprisingly, few expenditure items are absolutely fixed in even the short term -- an academic year.

As expected, transportation systems in high density districts are somewhat cheaper to operate. The cost savings from density apparently outweigh higher cost-of-living schedules in these denser districts. These estimated coefficients imply deviations from the QMTC frontier equal to:

$$D = E - e^{(5.3 - 2 (.37))} TR^{.98} DN^{-.10} \qquad (1)$$

At the point of means, it costs the average school district \$142.72 to transport one student per year, while a district on the frontier provides the same service for only \$67.07. Normalizing by population of the school district, per capita deviations for the sample averaged \$11.52. On average, Kentucky was the most efficient of our states with a \$6.50 average per capita deviation. Texas was second at \$8.39, followed by Massachusetts at \$13.31, Michigan at \$15.25, and Maryland at \$16.50. New Mexico turned out to be the least efficient with an average per capita deviation of \$21.68.

Sink Analysis

Our data allow us to define three "sinks" which are only slightly different from those defined for public libraries:

H1 -- total wage bill, including wages, salaries, and fringe benefits

H2 -- nonwage operating expenditures, primarily fuel, maintenance, and repairs

H3 -- depreciation expenditures for purchased school bus fleet

On average, 33 percent of a school district's transportation expenditures go for wages, salaries, and fringes (H1), 50 percent go for H2, and 17 percent for H3. When measured as a percent of expenditures, an analysis of variance (ANOVA) shows significant variation across states in each of the sinks. Table 5.3 lists the average percent of expenditures, by state, going into each sink. Compared to public libraries, school bus transportation systems are much less labor intensive, in part because of our inclusion of depreciation costs but largely due to the predominance of fuel costs. This latter fact may explain some of the across state variation evidenced in Table 5.3 as Texas and Maryland (recall, Maryland has 24 large county-wide school districts) have larger nonwage operating expenditures relative to the other states.

Regressing deviations from the QMTC frontier on the three sinks permits us to assess at the margin which of the gross expenditure categories contributes most to increased deviations.

The results of the regression are reported in Table 5.4. Recall from Chapter 4 that these coefficients must be interpreted relative to the average expected effect of an additional dollar expenditure, since, by the construction of the frontier, the average district is inefficient, lying two estimated standard deviations above the frontier. Thus, if a school district spends an additional dollar, some of it will go to raising the unit costs of the output. Based upon the differences in slopes between the linearized (not logged) regression line and the QMTC frontier, this average expected effect is computed as \$.53; that is, for every additional dollar spent in the average school district, a district on the frontier needs only spend \$.53 to achieve the same output increase. Since the estimated coefficients on H1 and H2 are larger than this average expected effect while that on H3 is smaller, it suggests that expenditures on wages and on nonwage operating items are major contributors (at the margin) to increased deviations. As in the public library case, our data does not permit us to address the question of whether the low return on wages and nonwage operating costs results from districts paying higher than necessary prices, using higher than required factor ratios, or both. What it does suggest is that school bus transportation systems could be more efficient, that is, move closer to the frontier, by becoming more capital intensive -- a result which is similar to the findings in the previous chapter for public libraries.

TABLE 5.3
Average Percent Expenditures by State for Each Sink

State	H1	H2	H3
Kentucky	34.3	51.8	13.9
Maryland	23.2	63.0	13.8
Massachusetts	30.3	47.4	22.5
Michigan	40.9	43.0	16.1
New Mexico	N/A	N/A	19.9
Texas	29.4	53.3	17.3

Note: H1 -- total wage bill as a percent of operating plus depreciation expenditures; H2 -- total nonwage operating expenditures as a percent of total operating plus depreciation expenditures; H3 -- total depreciation expenditures as a percent of total operating plus depreciation expenditures.

TABLE 5.4
Coefficient Estimates for Marginal Productivity of Additional Expenditures by Budget Category

Budget Category	Coefficient	T-Value
H1 -- salaries and benefits	.69	23.40
H2 -- nonwage operating expenses	.89	91.65
H3 -- depreciation of bus fleet	.03	.46
Constant	-30,588.95	
R^2	.97	
n	1429	
Average Expected Effect at the Means	.53	

Determinant Analysis

We estimated an equation similar in structure to that used for public libraries in the previous section. A school district's deviation per capita from the density adjusted QMTC frontier was modeled as a function of demand related variables, supply conditions, and the grant formula, expressed as the local share proportion. As measures of the demand variables, we included per capita income, the percent of the district's population that is elderly (greater than 59 years of age), the percent of the district's population between 5 and 18 years of age (its school age population), the percent of the district's population greater than 14 years old with a college education, and finally a measure of the local tax price for school bus transportation. Recall, that the coefficient on this last variable is equal to one plus the price elasticity of demand and hence its estimate may be positive if demand for the service is inelastic. We would expect the other coefficients to be positive except that for the percent elderly. Most studies have shown that the elderly are less willing to support local public services and in particular education services. Supply conditions are controlled through the inclusion of a measure of the percent of students transported who are special or handicapped students (generally, such students cost considerably more to transport than the typical student) and the fraction of the district's transportation system that is district owned rather than contracted out. We do not include density since the frontier has already been adjusted for the population densities of the school districts. Finally, the grant parameter is the local share (proportion) of total revenues.

The regression results are reported in Table 5.5. Since the log-log specification was used, all regression coefficient estimates are elasticities. The coefficients on the key variables conform to expectations; however, those on income and elderly have the "wrong" signs based upon standard demand theory. As expected, it costs more to transport special or handicapped students, and those districts with a larger percent of their populations of school age (and hence with a stronger interest in the education system) demand higher levels of service quality. The estimated price elasticity is equal to -.59 making school bus transportation slightly more inelastic than public libraries. Interestingly, it appears that contracted systems are less efficient than district owned. This is opposite the general concensus in the literature which finds private contractors to be cheaper and more effective than public provision for many local services. (See Kemper and Quigley, 1975, and Bails, 1979, for example.) This may be a spurious relationship reflecting the fact that many local school districts rely upon private contractors to transport the more costly students including those requiring interdistrict busing arrangements and special or handicapped students.

TABLE 5.5
Regression Estimates of the Determinants of the Deviations from the QMTC Frontier

Independent Variables	Coefficient	T-Value
Demand related:		
Tax price $(1 + \epsilon)$	.413	20.10
Median income	-.091	2.16
Percent school age population	.374	4.58
Percent elderly	.064	2.26
Percent population with college education	.010	.41
Supply conditions:		
Proportion district owned	.038	6.32
Percent special ed./handicapped	.012	3.41
Grant related:		
Local share	-.276	11.20
Constant	1.421	
F-Value	74.88	
R^2	.32	
n	1317	

The negative coefficient on the local share variable again suggests, under the proper assumptions explained in Chapter 3, the presence of information, incentive, or possibly distortion effects. The estimated elasticity of -.28 is remarkably close to the result found for public libraries, -.34. At the point of means, a 10 percent increase in local share will reduce per capita deviations from the QMTC frontier by $.74. The average school district, with a population of 20,171, will realize a savings of $14,926 or 4.62 percent of its operating plus depreciation expenditures. This compares with an increase of $15,544.95 in local burden associated with the 10 percent rise in local share. Hence, the loss of $15,544.95 in intergovernmental aid can be almost entirely offset by the potential efficiency gains associated with the increase in local share. As with public libraries, a reduction in state aid has the effect of increasing local share which, in turn, makes the district more efficient. The magnitude of these effects for school bus transportation systems is apparently so large as to render the loss in intergovernmental aid virtually costless to the average district.

TABLE 5.6
Effect of a $10,000 Lump Sum Increase in State Aid on Total Expenditure, Local Share, and Deviation from the QMTC Frontier

τ	Increase in Total Expenditure	Change in Local Share	Increase in Total Deviation	Increase in Deviation as Percent of Increase in Total Expenditure
0	0	-.031	$9,648	–
.20	$2,000	-.027	8,403	420
.40	4,000	-.023	7,158	179
.60	6,000	-.019	5,913	99
.80	8,000	-.015	4,669	58
1.00	10,000	-.011	3,423	34

τ is the increase in total expenditure resulting from a dollar increase in state aid.

Next we consider the situation in which a state provides additional aid in the form of a $10,000 lump sum grant to each of its school districts. As was the case with public libraries, the $10,000 lump sum grant may elicit a reduction of $10,000 in local revenues if there is complete substitution (τ = 0 in Table 5.6), a reduction of less than $10,000 if there is partial substitution ($0 < \tau < 1$ in Table 5.6), or no substitution ($\tau = 1$ in Table 5.6). In Table 5.6 we see that the local response for $\tau < 1$ increases a school district's deviation from the QMTC frontier.

As with public libraries, we consider the case where $\tau = .40$, which corresponds to a local response that is consistent with estimates found in Gramlich and Galper (1973). For $\tau = .40$, a \$10,000 lump sum grant will increase operating plus depreciation expenditures by \$6,000. This will reduce the fraction local share in Table 5.6 by .023. This decrease in local share will increase per capita deviations by \$.35 and total deviations by \$7,158 for the average school district in the sample. Therefore, the drop in local share will result in an increase in inefficiency (deviations from the frontier) that is 79 percent larger than the increase in total spending generated by the intergovernmental aid. In fact, only for values of τ greater than .60 will the spending increase outweigh apparent increases in inefficiency.

SUMMARY

The results for school bus transportation are remarkably similar to those of public library systems. The estimated elasticities are virtually identical implying that intergovernmental aid has quantitatively similar impacts in the two sectors. We do not want to make too much of the closeness of the elasticity estimates (indeed, we were quite surprised ourselves by the similarity). Rather, we wish to emphasize both the directions and magnitudes of the estimates as evidence of the disturbing impact of intergovernmental aid on local operating efficiencies and as confirmation of the hypothesized incentive and information effects associated with grants-in-aid. The policy implications of our findings are discussed in the next chapter.

6

RESEARCH AND POLICY

The empirical findings presented in the last two chapters support the contention that state grants-in-aid to local governments undermine the efficiency with which localities produce and deliver public services. But rather than close the book on this subject, the results raise many questions for future research and policy deliberations and hence represent what we hope is a definitive beginning rather than an end to this particular line of inquiry. In this last chapter, we would like to outline certain elements of a future research agenda, and to speculate on what changes in public policy may be appropriate in response to the discovered counterproductive effects of the current system of grants-in-aid.

FURTHER RESEARCH

The present study has been relatively modest in size and scope, and like any good scientific effort which claims new findings, it should be scrutinized and followed up in certain ways. We classify such follow-up in terms of three categories: replication, microanalysis of effects, and extension of findings.

Replication

We believe that much of the strength of our findings lies in the fact that very similar results have emerged independently from the analysis of two very different local public services -- libraries and school bus transportation -- produced by different classes of local government under widely varying grant-in-aid programs. Nonetheless, it seems the better part of wisdom that these findings be independently verified by other researchers, for these same services and possibly for other local services as well.

The latter, however, will be a formidable and/or expensive task. There are very few local services for which all the required elements fall into place for an analysis of grant-in-aid efficiency effects, as we have presented here. Such a "guinea pig" service needs to be describable in terms of a relatively simple and straightforward yet credible output measure, data must be available on this output measure, the cost-relevant differences in production conditions must be known, the service must be aided at a variety of levels across different states and localities, and quality variations, joint products, or joint accounting arrangements with other services must not be so overwhelming as to make corrections for these factors impossible. School transportation and public libraries seem to be unusual in these respects, although through major investments in data collection other local services may also be amenable to such analyses.

Micro-Analysis of Results

The studies of school transportation and public library services reveal a remarkably consistent estimate of approximately -0.3 for the elasticity of inefficiency (deviations from the quasi minimum total cost frontier) with respect to grants-in-aid (local share of service revenues). However, our model is not sufficiently precise, nor is available data sufficiently fine, to completely disentangle the various theoretical effects or mechanisms that lead to this result. Two aspects of this issue may be subject to further study through properly designed research efforts -- the distortion effect and fiscal illusion.

Distortion Effects

Of all the hypothesized ways in which grants have been seen to influence the productive efficiency of local government services, the distortion effect is the one economists should be most comfortable with. Essentially, distortion simply reflects the notion that local governments respond to effective changes in prices of inputs or intermediate outputs and they probably do this whether or not they try their utmost to be (locally) efficient. Conceptually, therefore, it seems a straightforward matter to confirm such behavior, if the proper data can be found and collected. There are two main requirements for such data. First, a service must be found that is aided by formulas in some states that are distortionary in a clearly discernible way. Public libraries seem a poor candidate in this respect because aid is generally provided through lump sum programs or through combinations of aid for different types of inputs so that the particular type of distortion that one should expect is not clear. School bus transportation, on the other hand, is more hopeful as there are a number of states for which aid is provided in a relatively straightforward way by the bus, the route mile, the driver, and so on (Dalton, 1980). There are also a substantial number of other states which provide straightforward matching or reimbursement programs that do not appear overtly distortionary, and these could be used for comparative purposes. Unfortunately, the data collected for the present study is not rich enough to undertake such an analysis, but with some investment in primary data collection it does seem feasible.

A specific study of distortion effects would have to hold constant the overall proportions of state versus local revenues in order to control for incentive, informational, and supervision effects, and would have to investigate whether there are differences among localities in the nature of expenditures and the overall levels of inefficiency corresponding to formula incentives. For example, holding all other things equal, do localities in states which reimburse transportation by the mile tend to have more circuitous routes? Do localities in states which reimburse by the bus tend to have more buses and have lower load factors or utilization rates? Are localities which are reimbursed by the driver more labor intensive? To the contrary, do localities in states which pay by the output unit, that is, a fixed price or reimbursement per student transported, operate more efficiently? And do localities in states which reimburse in a nondistortionary way (for example, by matching overall expenditures) operate more efficiently than localities in states that subsidize particular inputs, given the same overall proportions of subsidization? These questions seem amenable to separate empirical testing, given a sufficient investment in primary data collection. Moreover, the investment would seem quite worthwhile given the direct implications for state aid formula design contained therein.

Fiscal Illusion Effects

For both school bus transportation and public libraries, we have estimated the compound grant parameter $\eta + \pi$ at a value of approximately -0.3, and we have interpreted this as an inefficiency effect due to state aid. Recalling the discussion in the latter part of Chapter 3, this result falls into the "inelastic" category for which the latter interpretation depends upon the assumption that fiscal illusion among local citizens is high, that is, that local citizens have a poor perception of the presence of external aid funds; that is, in quantitative terms, we assume that $\eta = 0$.

Given the critical nature of this assumption, however, it would seem prudent to undertake some direct empirical research on the fiscal illusion phenomenon. None of the fiscal illusion literature in the field of public choice economics has attempted to do this (for example, see Wagner, 1976); rather, that research has proceeded by characterizing those factors that should lead to fiscal illusion, for example, the multiplicity of revenue sources, and then determining if local citizens tend to demand more services, or more precisely, more service expenditure, as fiscal illusion increases (that is, as fiscal illusion reduces the perceived though not actual tax-price). Interestingly, this literature is subject to similar criticism as the traditional microeconomic analyses of grants-in-aid as discussed in Chapter 2. In particular, the fiscal illusion literature also assumes that increased expenditures represent increased services rather than greater inefficiency. In any case, it would appear that a more direct investigation of the fiscal illusion phenomenon is justified. This would take the form of some type of survey research which would ask, in effect, what local citizens really know about the sources and magnitudes of revenues for local services, in particular the presence of grant-in-aid programs from the state and federal governments. Such research would help confirm the assumptions upon which the present conclusions regarding the relationship of grants to inefficiency have been reached.

Extension

The empirical studies represented in earlier chapters focus specifically on the effects of state grants on the efficiency of local government services. The concepts underlying the model upon which these effects have been estimated, however, are more general than that. In particular, we may anticipate that similar effects apply with respect to federal aid to states. The transfer of such conclusions is not automatic, however. In certain ways, states are fundamentally different from localities and hence may not behave in quite the same ways. To take the obvious differences, states are much larger and more politically diverse aggregations than localities. Moreover, states often act as fiscal intermediaries rather than as direct service providers, in some contrast to local governments. Such differences in part suggest that states may be even more prone to the inefficiency effects of grants, since their greater remoteness from individual citizens compounds the informational effects, making their officials even less accountable to those citizens. On the other hand, one might argue that states are so remote and unaccountable to begin with, that variations in the sources of their revenues would make no discernible difference. That is, grant-in-aid effects may be lost amidst the general insensitivity to local voter influences. Or, the federal government may be more, or less, effective than states as a monitor of grant programs, thus affecting the supervision component of the accountability phenomenon for states.

The only way to resolve this question is to carry out a program of empirical research on federal grant programs similar to what we have done here for state to local grant programs. Such a program would face the same problems we have had to cope with in the present study. Services must be found which can be characterized in terms of simple but comprehensive and documented output measures, quality variations (and joint products) must be minimal and/or subject to experimental or statistical control, uniform expenditures and output data must be available, and variations must exist in the level of aid distributed to different states. Furthermore, aid would have to be allocated in a manner which is not confounded with the demand parameters used in the model to control for (demanded) variations in quality of services. (For example, aid levels should not be highly correlated with state income levels.)

Not many federal programs meet these conditions. One which seems to come close is the Aid to Families with Dependent Children (AFDC) program. In this case, the output measure is simply the number of dollars transferred to eligible program beneficiaries. Inefficiency may take the form of higher administrative costs, high rates of error in payments to ineligible beneficiaries, or overpayments to eligibles. Quality variations seem negligible (a dollar is a dollar) despite the fact that states may choose to provide different benefit levels. Finally, aid levels do vary significantly among states, and although these aid levels are keyed to state demographic variables which may be correlated with the demand for quality parameters, this might be safely ignored since one could argue that quality variations would be negligible in this case. (This is a complex issue, however, which needs careful deliberation. For example, the timeliness of payments and mistakes in failing to service eligible clients may have to be considered.) However difficult the extension of empirical research into the domain of federal programs might be, it is clearly an important area for future investigation. The Reagan administration, for example, has proposed massive redirection of responsibilities for grants-in-aid programs, from the federal government to the states, justified partly on grounds related to efficiency (Peterson, 1984). Such proposals ought to be based on solid empirical research rather than conjecture or casual empiricism.

POLICY

Despite the value of continued empirical research into the productive inefficiency phenomena associated with grants-in-aid, the results already in hand are sufficiently strong to warrant consideration, particularly at the state to local level, of alternative policies aimed at ameliorating these effects. As indicated in Chapters 4 and 5, if our assumptions are correct, the magnitude of inefficiency impacts may be large enough to virtually wipe out any increases in output intended by policies of grant-in-aid financing. Effects of such magnitude are serious enough to lead to the consideration of major changes if not replacement of the current grants-in-aid system. Below, we consider such alternatives in these two basic categories: modifications to the present grants system, and alternatives to grants-in-aid financing of local services.

Modifications

There are at least three different ways in which current grant-in-aid systems might be modified or fine-tuned in a manner which preserves the basic structure and policy objectives. These alternative strategies may be labeled: productivity incentives, elimination of distortions, and improving the efficacy of supervision.

Productivity Incentives

As noted previously, some states have attempted to build incentives for improving the productive efficiency of local programs directly into state aid formulas. Notably, this has occurred in the federal and state welfare and medical aid programs wherein states, including New York, California, and Tennessee, have tied error rates in these programs to local payments of various kinds (Buechner and Schlageter-Chady, 1981). Another example of this idea is to tie state aid directly to a measure of output, that is, payment of a flat rate per unit of output. In such cases recipient localities have an incentive to maximize output and produce it as efficiently as possible so that any deficits are minimized and surpluses retained. In the pupil transportation area, several states, among them Alabama, Arkansas, Florida, Kansas, Kentucky, Oklahoma, Indiana, and Minnesota, pay at least part of their state aid according to the number of students transported to school (Dalton, 1980).

It is possible to view such output-oriented payment systems as a kind of "constructive distortion" arrangement intended to induce localities to focus their resources on intended outputs rather than other expenditure uses. Such a system is possible, of course, only where outputs are easily measured and succeed in capturing the most important aspects of service provision. The potential areas of application are not as restricted as it might first appear, however. In addition to school transportation, such aid formulas have been experimented with for public transportation in general, and in elementary and secondary education (in New York) and higher education (in Tennessee) (Buechner and Schlageter-Chady, 1981). Given that education absorbs half of all state aid, application of the output principle in this area could be dramatic in scope if not effect.

Eliminating Distortionary Formulas

As suggested earlier, aid formulas which distort the prices of inputs or alternative production strategies are common and commonly blamed for inducing inefficiencies in service delivery. They are also easily eliminated by moving to lump sum or general expenditure matching or reimbursement systems, or to (constructively distortionary) output payment systems. If research of the kind suggested earlier in this chapter confirms the importance of distortionary effects, then policies can be adopted to eliminate them. In most state aid programs states can copy from one another. If distortion proves to be an important effect, those states with nondistortionary formulas can lend the benefits of their experiences to those who may wish to adopt their policies.

In the context of movement towards nondistortionary formulas, it is important to recognize the recent trend of intergovernmental aid programs, noted in Chapter 1, away from categorical aid programs and towards block grant and general revenue sharing arrangements. These latter formulations can be argued to be even less distortionary than categorical programs which avoid discriminating on inputs, since these programs also avoid discriminating in terms of particular program strategies and technologies, or in the case of general revenue sharing, among different types of services altogether. For example, a block grant program in the realm of child welfare can be used to fund preventive as well as residential foster care services equally easily, while categorical aid programs have historically favored the former over the latter.

It might also be argued that block grant and revenue sharing arrangements would have other types of potentially productive efficiency effects. For example, although a block grant would lower local share in the same way as a categorical grant, it might have a less drastic effect than say a matching program because at the margin the price of additional local expenditure is higher in the former case than in the latter. Hence, local citizens might have a greater incentive to scrutinize incremental expenditures. Moreover, block grants may simplify the revenue system by consolidating separate aid flows, making informational problems less serious and easing the ability of the local citizenry to maintain accountability. On the other hand, more generalized state aid might make it easier for officials to manipulate funds, thereby making it harder to trace exactly how such dollars are being used. In this way, informational problems might be aggravated rather than relieved.

In sum, while the elimination of distortionary aid formulas seems to make good conceptual sense, the extension to block grants and general revenue sharing appears to require considerable additional research before conversion to these systems can be accepted without reservation on productive efficiency grounds.

Tightening Supervision

The one major hypothesized productivity effect of grants-in-aid which operates in the direction of improvement in local service efficiency is the possibility that oversight by the state may serve to increase the accountability of local officials and/or to induce those officials to adopt more efficient methods recommended by the state. While our empirical findings do not support the thesis that state supervision currently has this effect, it is not at all clear that states _could_ not exert a constructive influence of this kind. Indeed, it is generally the case that state auditing and monitoring procedures have not been oriented towards gauging and scrutinizing performance and efficiency, but rather have focused on whether funds have been spent legally, that is, in the manner specified by law according to procedures specified in program regulations. This leaves considerable room for improvement via the expansion of program evaluation, cost analysis, and monitoring activities by the state, functions which could ultimately improve the efficacy of the state as a supervisor of grant programs. Moreover, the issue of auditing frequency is one that must be examined carefully. Effective supervision requires not only that the right questions be asked, the right calculations performed, and the appropriate comparisons made between one recipient locality and another, but that such oversight be carried out often enough to warrant local officials' vigilance. While practices vary considerably from state to state and program to program, formal auditing commonly occurs substantially less frequently than annual appropriation and budgeting procedures. Typically, for instance, a subset of localities is selected for audit each year, leaving any given jurisdiction free from audit for several years running.

Whether increased investment in performance evaluation and monitoring by the state could be made to pay off in terms of increased efficiency of services financed through grants-in-aid is unknown. Very likely it will not, generally speaking, given the considerable costs of instituting effective procedures of this kind and the inherent difficulties of actually measuring output in many service areas. But this does seem to be an area worthy of further exploration to determine for which particular services such improvements may have effective application.

Alternatives

Patching up the existing structures of grants-in-aid has the distinct advantage of not explicitly raising, and hence calling into consideration, the underlying policy objectives of intergovernmental revenue programs. As summarized in Chapter 1, grant-in-aid systems have been intended to address several basic public policy goals, notably the internalizing of interjurisdictional externalities or benefit spillovers, the reconciling of fiscal disparities among localities or states and between alternative levels of government, and the redressing of distributional inequities among various groups of citizens. It is certainly questionable whether the present system of grants-in-aid succeeds in solving these problems very well. Nonetheless, any proposal to replace the grant system with some other regime must take these considerations into account.

For example, simply eliminating grants-in-aid seems likely to aggravate current fiscal disparities among localities and among states, and between state, local, and federal levels of government. On the other hand, redistributional considerations at the individual level are dealt with directly by income transfer programs, which could be even more effective in doing so if administered uniformly by the federal government. Moreover, it is unclear what would happen on the front of interjurisdictional spillovers. In general, such spillovers are very difficult to document and hence to determine whether grants effectively ameliorate them. It is highly possible, as Break (1980) suggests, that interlocal and interstate bargains and agreements might very well cope with benefit spillovers as effectively as a centrally administered system of grants-in-aid. In summary, therefore, it seems likely that simple elimination of intergovernmental aid programs could very well improve productive efficiency, but at the cost of exaggerating many of the interjurisdictional (horizontal and vertical) disparities that system was intended to deal with.

A more viable option might be to eliminate the "marble-cake" structure of public services financing by assigning both the financing and the delivery of various services to the same level of government. Thus, if particular services involve no serious benefit spillovers or fiscal disparities such services could comfortably be assigned to local government. If important interlocal disparities or benefit spillovers were involved, grants-in-aid might simply be replaced by complete state takeover of service finance and delivery. Similarly, if such disparities and inequities obtained among states, federal takeover could be entertained.

Such consolidation of financing and delivery in the same level of government would have the advantage of mitigating the "other people's money" syndrome at least to the extent that the citizens of the jurisdiction in question would face the whole costs of efficiency losses (or the full benefit of gains) and would therefore have greater incentives to hold their officials accountable. On the other hand, consolidation would probably mean a general movement in the responsibility of service delivery from lower to higher levels of government. This in itself may entail a loss of accountability, as upper levels of government tend to be larger, less scrutable, and more highly subject to indifference on the part of local citizens. In addition, states would probably prove themselves to be less adaptable to local cost and delivery conditions. For example, they may use pay scales out of line with local labor markets or they may use standard methods of production not well accommodated to local terrain or clientele (for example, methods of transportation, deployment of administrative or outreach offices, and so on). On the other hand, states can take advantage of certain economies of scale, systems of standardization, or monopsony in the purchase of inputs to production. It is very unclear what the net effect of this proposal on productive efficiency would be. One way to find out would be to make appropriate comparisons now in service areas where some states do, in fact, administer their own services. In school bus services, for example, a few states such as Georgia and South Carolina run their own systems. In AFDC also, there is a variety of practices with a number of states assuming direct responsibility for provision (within the framework of federal grants) rather than passing the responsibility for delivery down to the counties. Careful comparative analyses among such jurisdictions may yield further insights into the efficacy of state takeover as a strategy for coping with the productive inefficiency of intergovernmental aid systems.

A more promising, although more radical type of proposal would be to redirect economic resources in some way, so that local jurisdictions are capable of taxing themselves equitably for the purpose of producing the services they need. This could be done by having higher levels of government (presumably the federal government) redistribute resources to individuals in such a manner as to equalize the (fiscal) abilities of the localities they live in to raise revenues for local services. Interestingly enough, most of the bureaucratic machinery for doing this is already in place. In particular, the federal systems of income taxation and income maintenance could be modified to take into account the residence of recipients so that benefits can be keyed to the fiscal capacities and service needs of those jurisdictions. Using these systems to redistribute resources to individuals in this manner would then allow local jurisdictions to tax these benefits. Since local services would then be provided through local taxation, the losses of accountability from intergovernmental aid financing would be eliminated and greater productive efficiency may result.

Moreover, such a system would directly address the various fiscal disparity and inequity objectives of grant-in-aid programs. Only the interjurisdictional benefit spillovers might remain a problem, although as indicated earlier the seriousness of this repercussion, or the degree to which this could not be dealt with through direct interjurisdictional negotiations, remains questionable.

A system of redistribution to individuals and local taxation would have another possible benefit as well. It would set up an incentive for individuals to live in less well endowed localities where income tax rates would be lower and redistributive benefits higher. If such a system could be properly policed, for example, if people can be trusted or induced to correctly report their places of residences rather than use false addresses, then this incentive in itself would tend to reduce interjurisdictional fiscal disparities and service needs.

No doubt there are constitutional issues involved in bringing about such a regime. For while discrimination among individuals on the basis of where they live is a clearly established principle on the expenditure side of federal government operations, it has not been accepted on the tax side of the ledger. Still, it seems worthy of serious consideration, especially as it would be consistent both with the decentralization of authority as envisioned by the new federalists, the redressing of inequities which have long been the concern of social progressives, and with those conservatives and pragmatists presently worried about the decline of productivity in the public sector (Savas, 1982).

FINAL WORD

Hopefully, the last two decades of the twentieth century will be ones of prosperity for the United States. In view of the performance of the domestic economy in the 1970s and early

1980s, however, this prospect is by no means certain. It is clear, though, that the economy as a whole must become more efficient if it is to compete in the turbulent world economy. The public sector is an important part of this picture, perhaps an increasingly important part in future years. Savings that can be made in providing public services more economically and effectively will add to the ability of the economy as a whole to generate surpluses and to invest in the means for future production. Moreover, a more efficient public sector will help to inhibit the demise of confidence in government that can undermine any efforts to improve the quality of life to all citizens.

The grant-in-aid system has developed in the United States as an important element in social programs to address the pressing service needs of many different groups. No doubt this system has accomplished many of its social objectives. But this set of accomplishments seems to have come at a high cost. Nonetheless, the system cannot be tossed aside lightly. Any changes or replacements will have to ensure that equity be maintained and that essential services continue to be delivered. Still, it may now be time to consider such a change.

BIBLIOGRAPHY

Advisory Commission on Intergovernmental Relations (1980). "Recent Trends in Federal and State Aid to Local Governments," Report No. M-118, Washington, D.C.

Advisory Commission on Intergovernmental Relations (1981). "Significant Features of Fiscal Federalism, 1980-81 Edition," Report No. M-132, Washington, D.C.

Advisory Commission on Intergovernmental Relations (1984). "Significant Features of Fiscal Federalism, 1982-83 Edition," Report No. M-137, Washington, D.C.

Alexander, Kern, R. L. Johns, and K. Forbis Jordan (1971). Planning to Finance Education, National Educational Finance Project, Gainesville, Florida.

Anton, Thomas J. (1980). "Intergovernmental Change in the United States: Myth or Reality." Manuscript. Program in Urban and Regional Planning, University of Michigan, Ann Arbor.

Bails, Dale (1979). "Provision of Transportation Services." Public Choice, 34:1.

Beam, David R. (1978). "Economic Theory as Policy Prescription: Pessimistic Findings on Optimizing Grants," Advisory Commission on Intergovernmental Relations, Washington, D.C.

Brandon, D. David and Dennis R. Young (1978). "State Formula Grants and Productivity: A Concept Paper," New York State Commission on Management and Productivity in the Public Sector, Albany, New York.

Break, George R. (1980). Financing Government in a Federal System, The Brookings Institution, Washington, D.C.

Briggs, Ronald and David Venhuizen (1976). "Characteristics and Costs of Pupil Transportation," Traffic Quarterly, 30, April, pp. 303-323.

Bruno, Margery Grennon (1980). "A Description of State Funding Formulas for Public Libraries", Working Paper Number W-80-08, Institute for Urban Science Research. State University of New York at Stony Brook.

Buechner, Betsy and Carol Schlageter-Chady (1981). "Productivity and State Aid Formulas," Institute for Urban Science Research, Working Paper Number W-81-05, State University of New York at Stony Brook.

Charnes, A., W. W. Cooper, and E. Rhodes (1978). "Measuring the Efficiency of Decision Making Units," European Journal of Operations Research, Vol. 2, No. 6, pp. 429-444.

Charnes, A., W. W. Cooper, and E. Rhodes (1981). "Evaluating Program and Managerial Efficiency: An Application of Data Envelopment Analysis to Program Follow Through," Management Science, Vol. 27, No. 6, pp. 668-697.

Chira, Susan (1982). "Putnam Asks President Why a Broader Bridge Costs Less," New York Times, June 1.

Cooper, John E. (1967). Elementary School Principalship, Charles E. Merrill Books, Inc., Columbus, Ohio.

Courant, Paul N., Edward M. Gramlich, and David L. Rubenfeld (1979). "The Stimulative Effects of Intergovernmental Grants: Or Why Money Sticks Where It Hits," in Peter Mieskowski and William Oakland (eds.), Fiscal Federalism and Grants-in Aid, The Urban Institute, Washington, D.C.

Cyert, Richard and James March (1963). A Behavioral Theory of the Firm, Prentice-Hall, New York.

Dalton, Patrice (1980). "A Survey of State Aid Programs for School Transportation," Working Paper Number W-80-13. Institute for Urban Science Research, State University of New York at Stony Brook.

Durman, Eugene C., Barbara A. Davis, and Randall R. Bovbjerg (1984). "Block Grants and the New Federalism: The Second Year Experience," Draft No. 3076-01, The Urban Institute, April.

Ellwood, John W. (ed.), (1982). Reductions in U.S. Domestic Spending, Transaction Books.

Farrell, M. L. (1957). "The Measurement of Productive Efficiency," Journal of the Royal Statistical Society, Vol. 120, Sec. A., pp. 253-290.

Featherston, E. Glenn and D. P. Culp (1965). Pupil Transportation, Harper & Row, New York.

Getz, Malcolm (1980a). "Efficiency in Public Libraries: A Case Study of the Branches of the New York Public Library." Unpublished paper, Vanderbilt University, Nashville, TN.

Getz, Malcolm (1980b). Public Libraries: An Economic View, Johns Hopkins University Press, Baltimore.

Grennon, Margery (1981). "Public Library System Funding Formulas for the 50 States," Working Paper Number W-81-05, Institute of Urban Science Research, State University of New York at Stony Brook.

Gramlich, Edward M. (1977). "Intergovernmental Grants: A Review of the Empirical Literature," in Wallace Oates (ed.), The Political Economy of Fiscal Federalism, Lexington Books, D. C. Heath and Co., Lexington, MA.

Gramlich, Edward M. (1981). "Intergovernmental Grants," in Benefit-Cost Analysis of Government Programs, Prentice-Hall, Englewood Cliffs, New Jersey.

Gramlich, Edward M. and Harvey Galper (1973). "State and Local Fiscal Behavior and Federal Grant Policy," Brookings Papers on Economic Activity, Vol. I, Washington, D.C.: Brookings Institution.

Hale, George E. and Marian Lief Palley (1981). The Politics of Federal Grants, Congressional Quarterly Press.

Hirschman, Albert O. (1970). Exit, Voice, and Loyalty, Harvard University Press, Cambridge, Mass.

Howitt, Arnold M. (1984). Managing Federalism: Studies in Intergovernmental Relations, Congressional Quarterly Press.

Huang, Cliff J. and William M. Crosswhite (1979). "Production Efficiency Measurement: A Case Study of Michigan Telefarms." Mimeo, Department of Economics, Vanderbilt University, Knoxville, TN.

Improving State Aid to Public Libraries (1977). Prepared by the Government Studies and System, National Commission on Libraries and Information Science.

Johns, R. L. (1978). The Funding of School Transportation in Tennessee, Educational Finance and Management Institute, Gainesville, Florida.

Jordan, K. Forbis and Kern Alexander (1975). Financing the Public Schools of Indiana, Institute for Educational Finance, Gainesville, Florida.

Jordan, K. Forbis and Carol E. Hanes (1978). "A Survey of State Pupil Transportation Programs," School Business Affairs 44, May, pp. 133-34.

Jordan, K. Forbis and Nelda H. Cambron-McCabe (eds.), (1981). Perspectives in State School Support Programs, Ballinger Publishing Company, Cambridge, Massachusetts.

Kemper, Peter and John Quigley (1975). The Economics of Refuse Collection, Ballinger Publishing Company, Cambridge, Massachusetts.

Lane, Rodney et al. (1982). The Funding of Public Library Services in Indiana: An Examination of the Existing State System of Support and Feasible Alternatives. Philadelphia: University City Sciences Center.

Leibenstein, Harvey (1966). "Allocative Efficiency vs. X-Efficiency," American Economic Review, June.

Library Statistics: A Handbook of Concepts, Definitions, and Terminology, (1966), American Library Association, Chicago.

Luce, Thomas and Janet Rothenberg Pack (1984). "State Support Under the New Federalism," Journal of Policy Analysis and Management, Vol. 3, No. 3, Spring.

March, James and Herbert Simon (1958). Organizations, John Wiley and Sons, New York.

McDougall, Gerald A. (1980). Expenditure Effects of Grants-in-Aid to Local Governments: Fundability -- Parts I and II, prepared for the U.S. Department of Housing and Urban Development, April.

McGuire, Martin (1978). "A Method for Estimating the Effect of a Subsidy on the Receiver's Resource Constraint: With an Application to U.S. Local Governments 1964-71," Journal of Public Economics 10, pp. 25-44.

McGuire, Martin (1979). "An Econometric Model of Federal Grants and Local Fiscal Response," in Peter Mieskowski and William Oakland (eds.), Fiscal Federalism and Grants-in-Aid, The Urban Institute, Washington, D.C.

Melcher, Thomas R. (1981). "State Pupil Transportation Programs," in K. Forbis Jordan and Nelda Cambron-McCabe (eds.), Perspectives in State School Support Programs, Ballinger Publishing Company, Cambridge, Massachusetts.

Mieskowski, Peter and William Oakland (eds.), (1979). Fiscal Federalism and Grants-in-Aid, The Urban Institute, Washington, D.C.

Molz, Kathleen (1976). Federal Policy and Library Support, Cambridge: MIT Press.

Nathan, Richard P., and Fred C. Doolittle (1984). "Overview: Effects of the Reagan Domestic Program on States and Localities," Princeton Urban and Regional Research Center, The Woodrow Wilson School, Princeton University, June.

Nielsen, Waldemar (1979). The Endangered Sector, Columbia University Press, New York.

Niskanen, William (1971). Bureaucracy and Representative Government, Aldine Publishing Co., New York.

Oates, Wallace (1977). The Political Economy of Fiscal Federalism, Lexington Books, D. C. Heath and Co., Lexington, MA.

Olson, Gerald and G. Ross Stephens (1979). "Financing State and Local Services and the Interflow of Funds in the United States, 1957 to 1977: Vols. I and II," University of Missouri, Kansas City.

Ozmon, Howard and Sam Craver (1972). Busing: A Moral Issue, Phi Delta Kappan Educational Foundation, Bloomington, Indiana.

Peterson, George E. (1982). "The State and Local Sector," in L. Palmer and Isabel V. Sawhill (eds.), The Reagan Experiment, The Urban Institute Press.

Peterson, George E. (1984), "Federalism and the States," in John L. Palmer and Isabel V. Sawhill (eds.), The Reagan Record, Cambridge: Ballinger.

Rose-Ackerman, Susan (1978). Corruption: A Study in Political Economy, Academic Press, New York.

Ross, John P. and Jesse Burkhead (1974). Productivity in the Local Government Sector, Lexington Books, Lexington, Mass.

Russell, Louise B. (1977). "Medical Care Costs," in Joseph A. Pechman (ed.), Setting National Priorities: The 1978 Budget, The Brookings Institute, Washington, D.C.

Savas, E. S. (1982). Privatizing the Public Sector, Chatham, N.J.: Chatham House Publishers.

Sexton, Thomas, Richard Silkman, and Andrew Hogan (1984). "Data Envelopment Analysis: Critique and Extensions," Harriman College, SUNY at Stony Brook, Discussion Paper.

Shera, Jesse H. (1965). Foundations of the Public Library, The Shoe String Press, Inc., Chicago.

Silkman, Richard H. and Dennis R. Young (1979). "The Impact of State Grants on the Efficiency of Local Government Service," Institute for Urban Science Research, Working Paper Number W-79-01, SUNY at Stony Brook, Stony Brook, NY.

Silkman, Richard and Dennis R. Young (1982). "X-Efficiency and State Formula Grants," National Tax Journal, Vol. XXXV, No. 3, September.

Silkman, Richard H. and Dennis R. Young (1983). "X-Efficiency, State Formula Grants, and Public Library Systems," in John Quigley (ed.), Perspectives on Local Public Finance and Public Policy, Vol. 1, JAI Press, pp. 195-222.

Skloot, Floyd (1978). "The Road is Long -- Problems in State Funding of Pupil Transportation Programs," Planning and Changing, 9, Spring, pp. 34-41.

State Government Finances in 1982 (1983), U.S. Department of Commerce, Bureau of the Census, U. S. Government Printing Office, Washington, D.C., October.

Statistical Abstract of the United States -- 1984 (1984), U.S. Department of Commerce, Bureau of the Census, Washington, D.C.

Stollar, Dewey H. (1971). "Pupil Transportation," in Alexander, et al. (eds.), Planning to Finance Education, National Education Finance Project, Gainesville, Florida.

Sunley, Emil M. Jr. (1976). "State and Local Governments," in Henry Owen and Charles L. Schultze (eds.), Setting National Priorities: The Next Ten Years, The Brookings Institution, Washington, D.C.

Wagner, Richard E. (1976). "Revenue Sharing, Fiscal Illusion, and Budgetary Choice," Public Choice, 25, pp. 45-61.

Williamson, Oliver (1964). The Economics of Discretionary Behavior: Managerial Objectives in a Theory of the Firm, Prentice-Hall, New York.

Winer, Stanley L. (1979). "Some Evidence of the Effect of the Separation of Spending and Taxing Decisions," Carleton Economic Papers, 80-81, Carleton University, Ottawa, Canada.

Young, Dennis R. (1978). "Productivity Effects of State Formula Grants," Paper presented to the Public Choice Society, New Orleans, March, 1978.

INDEX

ABOUT THE AUTHORS

RICHARD H. SILKMAN is associate professor of public policy and management in the Public Policy and Management Program at the University of Southern Maine. He was previously on the faculty of the W. Averell Harriman College for Policy Analysis and Public Management of the State University of New York at Stony Brook, and has served and continues to serve as a consultant to a number of public and private organizations in the areas of intergovernmental relations, employment training, and economic regulation. Dr. Silkman received the B.S. degree from Purdue University and the M.A. and Ph.D. degrees from Yale University in economics.

DENNIS R. YOUNG is a professor in the W. Averell Harriman College for Policy Analysis and Public Management of the State University of New York at Stony Brook. He is also a visiting faculty member of the Institution for Social and Policy Studies, program on nonprofit organizations, at Yale University. Dr. Young received the B.E. degree from the City College of New York and the M.S. and Ph.D. degrees from Stanford University in Engineering-Economic Systems. His principal research interests are the economic organization of public services and the theory and management of nonprofit organizations. His books include How Shall We Collect the Garbage? A Study in Economic Organization, Foster Care and Nonprofit Agencies (co-authored with Stephen Finch), and If Not for Profit, For What? A Behavioral Theory of the Nonprofit Sector Based on Entrepreneurship.